Sorry...

Sorry...

the hardest word
and how to use it

max davidson

Constable • London

Constable & Robinson Ltd
3 The Lanchesters
162 Fulham Palace Road
London W6 9ER
www.constablerobinson.com

First published in the UK by Constable,
an imprint of Constable & Robinson Ltd, 2010

A copy of the British Library Cataloguing in
Publication Data is available from the British Library

ISBN: 978-1-84901-414-4

Printed and bound in the EU

1 3 5 7 9 10 8 6 4 2

PEFC
PEFC/16-33-111
CATG-PEFC-052

For Julia — with apologies for the English weather

acknowledgements

My thanks to Andreas Campomar and the rest of team at Constable & Robinson for helping me bring to fruition a project that has long been dear to my heart. Thanks, too, to Jonathan Pugh for his illustration on the cover.

Now might also be a good time to say sorry to all the people whom, in a long and error-strewn life, I have wronged, insulted, let down, fobbed off with cheap Christmas presents, forgotten to thank for dinner, kept waiting on street corners, bombarded with nuisance emails, failed to buy drinks, bought too many drinks, insulted for supporting Arsenal, abused for trying to sell me Sky-Plus, derided for voting Conservative, or simply called names which, in the cold light of day, I regret.

Apologies, in particular, to: Anna and Clara; the entire Gren family; Liz Hunt, Father Raphael Appleby, for losing touch; Sue and Paul, for enjoying Mozart; Graham Boynton and his cronies; Robert Rogers, for the April Fool that went wrong; my sister and brother-in-law; Beatrice Natzler, for forgetting her twelfth birthday; John and Erica Hedges, *passim*; Kathy Lette, for pinching one of her best puns; my mother, for having too many second helpings of pota-toes; Tina McBride; Graham Allen MP; Philip Ruttley, for thrashing him at chess; Liam and Sally, for That Article; Raymond Blanc, for criticising the braised oxtail at Le Manoir aux Quat' Saisons; Alison

Court, for not understanding what she saw in Haddenham; Sir Max Hastings, for cursing him; Vicki Tuck; Ann Winterton; that nice air hostess on the Qantas flight to Singapore, who deserved better; Clive Bennett, for calling him 'a diseased Belgian fantasist'; Kathryn Mead; the linesman who forgot to flag Drogba offside; Jo and Miles; Libby and Richard; Kenneth Branagh, for hating his Hamlet; Nicholas and Gillian Shakespeare, for not chilling the wine properly; Anthony Goff; Ursula Horsfall; Nick Clegg, for doubting him; and many, many others.

introduction

I'm sorry to start with a guilty confession, but how better to introduce a book about the lost art of apologising? Saying sorry is in my DNA. Part of my birthright, you might say. I am English, therefore I apologise. Sorry, but there it is. Americans kick ass. Frenchmen kiss each other. Englishmen grovel.

When I was fifteen, to my shame, I fell hook, line and sinker for one of the corniest movies ever to come out of Hollywood. Remember *Love Story*? Ali McGraw dying of cancer and Ryan O'Neal being big and brave and stiff-upper-lipped about it? I cried like a baby during the death-bed scene. And remember that cheesy piano score? Tum-ti-tum-tum-tum, tum-ti-tum-ti-tum . . . I went around humming it for weeks, tears welling in my eyes.

But I never understood – in fact, I actively distrusted – the strapline: 'Love means never having to say you're sorry.' What was that all about? As soon as I heard Ali McGraw say the line I screwed up my acne-flecked face in disapproval. Who had written this script? Walt Disney? It was a revolting doctrine. Not just revolting, dangerous. For if one never apologised, never admitted one was in the wrong, what chance was there of becoming a good person?

Never say sorry? But I loved saying sorry. For as long as I could remember I had used the s-word at every opportunity; to appease parents, teachers, friends and total strangers. The apologies did me good – like prunes or yoghurt. Boy Scouts did a good deed a day; I did a good grovel a day, beating myself up over the most footling misdemeanours.

I had been sent to a Catholic boarding school, so I was in thrall to the exhilarating roller coaster that was the confessional: contrition, followed by absolution, followed by an emotional buzz that could last for hours. Why abandon those habits because of a crappy one-liner in a Hollywood tear-jerker?

Years later, when I published my first novel, *The Wolf*, I made my rejoinder. Paul, my sexually errant hero, was forever in trouble with the women in his life and having to placate them. 'To Paul,' I wrote, in a sly echo of *Love Story*, 'love meant saying he was sorry, then waiting to be told what he was sorry for.' The joke was wasted on the critics, but for me it was a kind of *credo*.

To this day, like a man with Tourette's, I find myself saying sorry, times without number, often with no clear sense of what exactly I am apologising for. I believe in the s-word. Like 'please' and 'thank you', it makes the world go round.

I'm not seriously suggesting that people should apologise when they have done nothing wrong – that's just silly – but one thing I do know from long experience is that you never feel sorry for saying sorry, just as you never feel sorry for giving money to a beggar. Even if the word has just popped out – as it often does in my case – it seldom does any real harm.

Example: I am having a quiet coffee in my local café, reading a newspaper, minding my own business. A woman and her out-of-control child come careering past, bound for the loo. I have been watching the child out of the corner of my eye; he has a face like

Jack Nicholson, with a streak of tomato ketchup on his forehead, and has spent the last ten minutes grinding sugar lumps. Now, as he passes, he sends my coffee flying with his elbow. His mother gets coffee on her expensive-looking shoes. 'Sorry,' I say, without thinking. Absurd? Of course it is, but if I clipped the boy around the ear I would end up in court. Peace reigns. The mother insists on buying me another coffee, plus a large slice of chocolate cake. The manager of the café bestows a beatific smile on me. I am the hero of the hour.

Another example: I am meeting a woman at a restaurant for lunch. I am ten minutes early; she is forty minutes late. She makes to apologise and I pre-empt her. 'My fault. Must have got the time wrong. Sorry.' I take the blame because taking the blame is easier than not taking the blame. Just misplaced chivalry, some would say, but what is wrong with a bit of chivalry in our backbiting world? Lunch is amicable, when it could have opened on a sour note.

Knee-jerk apologies are as English as evensong and warm beer. Hard-bitten Americans and Australians are always bemused by the way that, if two Englishmen bump into each other in the street, they will both apologise, instantly, eagerly, as if trying to beat each other to the punch. It just doesn't happen that way in Manhattan or downtown Sydney. You are more likely to get a snarled 'Look where you're going'. In those more confident, more assertive societies, the instinct to blame runs deeper than the instinct to appease.

If there were Olympic medals for saying sorry, we English would win gold, silver and bronze, but – and hence this book – there is no point in pretending that all is well in the great world of English apology. We are not half as good at it as we were, and we are getting worse all the time. We still enjoy grovelling, but we fluff our lines. We prevaricate. We hedge our bets. We say sorry to the wrong person or at the wrong time. We consult lawyers when we should be writing our own scripts. We have gone all American and corporate, preferring portentousness ('I accept full responsibility for . . .') to the simple and heartfelt: 'I'm sorry.'

A nation with a genius for self-abasement has become a nation that, when it comes to apologising, does not know if it is coming or going. One minute we are howling for an apology from some B-list celebrity who is skulking in their house, besieged by reporters, because they are being pilloried for sleeping with another B-list celebrity; the next we are saying sorry *en masse*, like synchronised swimmers, for something that happened two hundred years ago.

As a society, we remain besotted with the s-word. It enjoys totemic status, binding the whole tribe together. 'Just say you're sorry' has become one of the drumbeats of the age. New apologies are demanded every day; from politicians, bankers, footballers and two-timing spouses. We tell ourselves that if only someone says sorry, everything will be all right and we can all live happily ever after. But how often is the apology that has been demanded forthcoming, and in a form that gives satisfaction to all concerned? It is a struggle to remember a single recent apology from a public figure that had the ring of truth – the norm is a half-baked apology for an apology, couched in weasel words that have been run past a lawyer.

For many, saying sorry has become as laborious as giving birth. In fact, if a single English word trips people up, bamboozles them, makes them perform undignified contortions in an effort to avoid using it, it is the s-word.

Our politicians are particularly culpable. For years they obstinately refused to apologise; saying sorry was seen as a sign of weakness – they took their cue from Benjamin Disraeli: 'Never explain, never apologise.' Only when they had done something heinous, like John Profumo lying to the House of Commons, did they display contrition before their peers. More recently, politicians discovered that a gracious apology made them look humble, self-critical – all the things voters liked.

It was best, other things being equal, to apologise for things that had happened before they were born. The slave trade was a good place to start: everyone felt so, so sorry for that. Tony Blair, ludicrously, apologised for the Irish potato famine, which was just about the only cock-up for which people *didn't* blame him. But saying sorry for Bloody Sunday, a quarter of a century after the event, was an apology too far for Mr Blair. Pity, a judicious use of the s-word might have saved the tax-payer £200 million – that being the cost of the public inquiry into Bloody Sunday, which was the political alternative to apologising. In cash terms, it was the most expensive non-apology in British history.

David Cameron, the heir to Tony Blair's brand of touchy-feely politics, cannot say sorry often enough. Unlike many politicians, he deploys the word easily, even enthusiastically. In late 2008, as the banking crisis escalated and apologies were demanded of bankers and finance ministers, Mr Cameron joined the party, apologising for Conservative economic policies. Who cared about Conservative economic policies? They were in opposition in 2008; they bore no responsibility for public finances. But the air was heavy with contrition and the Tory leader did not want to miss out.

Few political rows unfold nowadays without the s-word being invoked. There was a classic just-say-sorry spat in April 2009, when a Downing Street spin doctor was found to have sent defamatory emails about a Conservative backbench MP, Nadine Dorries. The Tories demanded an apology from Gordon Brown, who sent Mrs Dorries a letter expressing his 'regret' about the incident. 'Not good enough!' howled the Tories. 'Apologise properly!' Mr Brown capitulated. 'I'm sorry about what happened,' he told an interviewer, through gritted teeth, sending researchers scurrying to find the last time he had used the s-word in public. Never, said the cynics.

The absurd thing about the incident, symptomatic of what a tangle we get into over the s-word, is that Gordon Brown had not actually apologised at all. Yes, he had said sorry, as his critics had demanded, but not in a way that involved accepting responsibility for the behaviour of his staff. If he had said: 'I'm sorry *for* what happened', now that would have been a kosher apology. Being sorry *about* what happened was platitudinous guff.

In the last ten minutes alone I have been sorry about the fact that it is raining, sorry about the size of my gas bill and sorry about the fact that I have run out of coffee. But I have apologised for nothing. I know, as Gordon Brown knows, that there is a world of difference between sorry-sad and sorry-penitent. It is a clear distinction, semantically, but how many people appreciate that distinction when recriminations are flying and the just-say-sorry mob are baying for their pound of flesh?

The mob were at it again later in 2009, when a handwritten letter of condolence from Gordon Brown to the mother of a soldier killed in Afghanistan sparked a public outcry. The mother was livid that the prime minister had misspelt her name, Gordon Brown was mortified and rang to apologise, the *Sun* moved in for the kill like a pack of hyenas, and for the best part of forty-eight hours, the air was blue with s-words and people screaming for more s-words. Madness. People ended up feeling sorry for the man apologising. There, I have just used the s-word again, in another of its multifarious uses. Foreigners are bewildered that a single English word can crop up so often – and cause so much havoc.

The Hardest Word is my attempt to bring a little clarity into an area where feelings run high, ambiguities are rife and people trip themselves up quite unnecessarily. I shall look at the curious history of the s-word: one of those verbal bastards that started out meaning one thing, developed a secondary meaning, and now, more often than not, straddles both meanings in the most ungainly, infuriating way. Does its very slipperiness explain why the British, with their genius for saying one thing and meaning another, took the word to their hearts? And where does that leave us when it comes to apologising, *really* apologising, and not just paying lip service to the concept?

As a Catholic (sorry, lapsed Catholic) I still cleave to the doctrine of contrition I was taught as a boy. Saying sorry, of itself, meant nothing: it was just a word. Only by being sorry, genuinely contrite, resolved to do better next time, could one expect forgiveness. In the dusty teachings of theology, there is an intellectual rigour lacking in the just-say-sorry brigade, for whom apologising is a quick fix, a bit of feel-good flannel.

But it is one thing to feel contrite, quite another to put contrition into words, particularly if the words have been drafted by someone else. Apologising has been made ten times harder by lawyers, with their caveats. Two Englishmen bumping into each other may chorus 'Sorry! Sorry!', but if they are driving cars at the time they have been hard-wired *not* to say sorry, come hell or high water.

Saying sorry has also been made harder by the intransigence of those who refuse to apologise on principle. Two concurrent but contradictory trends can be discerned: a trend for apologising more and more, particularly for things like the slave trade, and, as a reaction to the first trend, matched with Newtonian precision, a trend for viewing all apologies as a form of emotional self-indulgence.

Britain is increasingly split into two opposing camps: quiet-lifers like me, the serial apologisers who think the s-word helps the world go round; and pig-headed pachyderms who detest the very sound of the word and worry that if they use it they will lose face with their neighbours and have to emigrate to New Zealand.

If knee-jerk apologies are absurd, obstinate non-apologies can be even more absurd. There is nothing sadder than the person who digs in their heels and refuses to say sorry unless the other person says sorry first. You see it every day – whether in football managers, mulishly convinced of their case, or in married couples, digging themselves deeper and deeper into their respective holes. They see saying sorry as a sign of weakness. It is nothing of the kind; it is a sign of self-confidence, emotional maturity and a proper sense of fairness.

To my utopian mind there are right and wrong ways of apologising, just as there are right and wrong ways of using apostrophes, cooking soufflés and riding bicycles. There have been some magnificent apologies over the years – my roll call of model apologisers will include David Beckham, Hugh Grant and Willy Brandt – but many more half-baked, insincere, unsatisfactory ones. I shall try to unpick what distinguishes a good apology from a dodgy one and, with apologies, obviously, for my temerity, try to suggest an etiquette of sorry-saying for the twenty-first century: when to grovel and, just as important, how to grovel.

Apologising graciously may seem like one of the more arcane life skills, but in our curmudgeonly, nit-picking society, we have never needed it more.

mr brown says sorry

On 11 September 2009, a signed article by Gordon Brown appeared in the *Daily Telegraph*. The then prime minister, trailing in the polls, wanted to say sorry for something that happened in 1952, when Mr Brown was one year old. For connoisseurs both of Gordon Brown and of the British fetish for apologising, it was quite a moment.

People will remember the Brown premiership for all sorts of reasons – some good, some bad – but it was certainly not an era when Downing Street was precipitate in admitting its mistakes. Mr Brown's guiding political philosophy was that Mr Brown was right. He would admit to the odd error of judgement, like the dropping of the 10p rate of income tax, but such admissions were so rare, and so begrudging, that they became collectors' items. As for saying sorry, it was just not the Gordon Brown style. I have already alluded to one occasion when he did use the s-word, after a Downing Street spin doctor had traduced a Tory backbencher, but that was mere political window-dressing: a non-apology cunningly disguised as the real McCoy.

The *Telegraph* article, by comparison, was steeped in genuine-sounding contrition, as if the events of 1952 had been nagging Mr Brown's conscience since he was a wee bairn in rompers in Kirkcaldy. What had been bothering him all those years – admittedly his memory had to be jogged by gay rights campaigners, Stephen Fry, a large pet-ition on the Downing Street website and the imminence of a general election – was the fate of Alan Turing, the Cambridge mathematician who cracked the Germans' Enigma code during the Second World War.

A great patriot, and also a homosexual, Turing was convicted of gross indecency in 1952 and confronted with a choice between prison and chemical castration. He chose the latter, but took his own life two years later. It was a deplorable episode, and the prime minister wanted to apologise for it. 'Turing's treatment was utterly unfair,' he wrote, 'and I am pleased to have the chance to say how sorry I am and we all are for what happened to him.'

To the purist, all this is industrial-strength hogwash. Not only was Mr Brown apologising for something that happened when he was one, he was presuming to apologise on behalf of everyone in the country, even those who thought homosexuality should still be a criminal offence. What possessed the prime minister to think he could speak for every man Jack of us? Also, if one is being really pedantic, why did he confine his apology to what happened to Alan Turing? Why not extend it to the thousands of other British homosexuals who suffered a similar fate during the same period? Getting an apology right on the money is harder than it seems.

But that does not mean it is not worth the effort.

One of my main contentions in this book is that a clumsy apology made with honourable intentions is better than no apology at all. Saying sorry can sometimes be no more than sympathetic mood music: making the right noises at the right time. How well the Turing apology meets that test is a question to which I shall return later.

It is interesting to compare Mr Brown's gauche attempt to ingratiate himself with the gay community with an earlier apology by David Cameron. 'I'm sorry for Clause 28,' Mr Cameron declared in July

2009. 'We got it wrong.' The Clause 28 in question was the infamous legislation, later repealed, which debarred local education authorities from promoting homosexuality in schools. It was enacted in May 1988 – when Mr Cameron was still at Oxford, probably drinking himself under the table at the Bullingdon Club at the very moment the House of Commons was waving through the Bill.

So how, quibbles the pedant, can he say sorry for Clause 28? The legislation was not his responsibility, it was the bastard brainchild of the Thatcher government, antediluvian in its attitude to homosexuals. But the pedant is missing the point: it is the four subsequent words that matter in this instance. 'We' – that is, the Conservatives, and Mr Cameron was speaking as leader of the party – 'got it wrong.' Simple, clear, unambiguous; they are probably the four words people most want to hear from their political leaders, but never do. There is a thrilling crispness to the apology that is in sharp contrast to the more ponderous breast-beating of Gordon Brown. Mr Cameron, as a good politician should, cuts to the chase.

Now that he is in Downing Street, Mr Cameron will find his skills as an apologiser put to a much sterner test. Colleagues will mess up and he will have to defend them in public, while being privately furious with them. He will make mistakes but not acknowledge them, for fear of giving ground to his opponents. When the honeymoon is over and the public become disenchanted with him, he will try to deflect their anger, rather than engage with it honestly. He will end up as opinionated and pig-headed and unrepentant as every other incumbent of his office, because that is what power does to politicians. In time, people may even look back and think, 'That nice Gordon Brown was so much humbler. He didn't think he was God, always right, never wrong.' Downing Street is not the ideal place to perfect the art of saying sorry.

But for now Mr Cameron, deservedly, enjoys the reputation of a good communicator and someone who says approximately what he means – something that Mr Brown, that tortured son of the manse, forgot how to do when he was a child. And in the arsenal of good communication skills the ability to know when and how to say sorry – defusing a situation instead of making it worse – is not a weapon to be underestimated.

Across the Atlantic, Barack Obama has also proved an adroit exponent of the s-word. His predecessor, President Bush, was so verbally challenged that he was never going to master a tricky word like 'sorry'. 'I'm sorry it's happening,' Mr Bush told a TV interviewer, when invited to apologise for leading America into recession. *It?* Could there be a clearer example of a politician saying sorry in general terms, but evading personal responsibility?

Mr Bush did no better when apologising for one of the low points of his presidency – the tardy response to Hurricane Katrina in 2005. 'To the extent that the federal government didn't fully do its job right, I take responsibility,' he admitted, nearly two years after the event. What a thin gruel of remorse. How cautious in its wording. How mean-spirited in tone. The apology does not tick a single one of the boxes that a good apology should.

Mr Obama, thus far, has been more gracious in admitting his mistakes. 'I screwed up,' he said simply, after one early blunder. Not a family-friendly choice of words, perhaps, but a disarmingly frank admission. After he had raised feminist hackles by calling a reporter 'sweetie', the president rang to leave an apologetic voicemail message: 'That's a bad habit of mine. I meant no disrespect and I am duly chastened.' After he had offended the disabled with a comment on a TV chat show, likening his bowling skills to something in the Special Olympics, he telephoned the Chairman of the Special Olympics from Air Force One and ate humble pie. It was an uncharacteristic blunder, but he atoned for it with commendable swiftness.

Such sure-footedness under pressure was par for the course for a relaxed, self-confident politician, comfortable in his own skin and good at making other people feel at ease. One expected Mr Obama to be good at saying sorry, in the same way that one expected him to be a good dancer when taking the floor at the Inauguration Balls.

A seemingly cerebral process – the selection of the right words – is actually a process that reveals the whole human being. A physically clumsy person is also likely to be a clumsy apologiser (I am looking at you, John Prescott), while grace of bearing often goes hand in hand with grace of expression.

The skill set of a successful politician changes from generation to generation. In 2010, whether they are naturally good, bad or indifferent at saying sorry, politicians face more demands to apologise than ever before. When something goes wrong, people want an explanation, and if the explanation does not hold water, they want heads to roll. Nothing is more guaranteed to cause a public outcry than a lack of contrition among people in high places. The bad old days, when the people in charge knew best because they were the people in charge, have gone. If people hold responsible positions they need to be held responsible. It is called democracy.

But, if politicians are expected to apologise more now than twenty years ago, that does not mean they have got better at doing it. Old habits die hard. 'Success has many fathers,' said President Kennedy, 'but failure is an orphan.' The worse the mess into which politicians have led us, the greater their tendency to pass the buck – and for connoisseurs of buck-passing, with nobody prepared to take ultimate responsibility for anything, the banking crisis of 2008–9 was a master class in the art.

There was a plethora of apologies – of a sort – from people admitting they had been at fault – up to a point – and could have done better – with hindsight. Half-apologies. Quarter-apologies.

Non-apologies masquerading as the real thing. Emotional apologies, drenched in crocodile tears. Lawyerly apologies. Apologies that had been crawled over for hours by PR companies. Apologies that had been composed in draft then circulated around six Whitehall departments before seeing the light of day. Apologies that sounded as if they had been written while drunk. Apologies that might as well have been delivered in Serbo-Croat. Apologies that sounded terrific, but were as phony as a seven-pound note. Hypocritical apologies. Self-serving apologies. And, last but not least, this masterpiece of obfuscation from the then Chancellor of the Exchequer, Alistair Darling:

> 'All of us have to have the humility to accept that, over the last few
> years, things got out of alignment.'

It is the contrast between the vagueness of 'things' and the precision of 'alignment' that makes this slithery non-apology such a gem. The speaker, remember, is the Chancellor of the Exchequer; he knows more about banking and how the banking crisis developed than 99.9 per cent of the people in the country. You can bet a subprime mortgage that there are mistakes which he made at the Treasury, and which he *knows* that he made, but as Mr Darling dons sackcloth and ashes and joins the queue of people taking their turn on the naughty step, his nerve fails him. He cannot name those mistakes. He dare not name those mistakes. He is definitely not going to use the s-word and have *that* on his political CV. So instead he clutches at the pitiful lifeline: 'things'.

Perhaps one should not be too harsh on Mr Darling. We have all found ourselves in similar situations: in the doghouse, contrite, chastened, keen to apologise, but unsure of the best form of words. 'Sorry' on its own is rarely enough, but as soon as one adds an explanatory rider it starts to look like an excuse. Apologising can be an elusive art.

6

If the banking crisis turned sorry-saying into a cottage industry, with everyone doing their own thing, mixing-and-matching protestations of regret, admissions of responsibility and vague promises to do better next time, those apologies were mere canapés compared with the banquet of contrition that followed the parliamentary expenses scandal.

It was like a Whitehall farce in which all the characters were caught with their trousers down at the same time. The public wanted to hear the s-word, so MPs obliged, rushing out hand-wringing press statements. Never were so many apologies issued by so many politicians in such a short space of time. But the apologies were so hollow and hypocritical that the public refused to accept them. 'YOU DON'T GET IT!' they roared, like an audience at a pantomime. So the MPs rushed out a second wave of apologies. They should have been an improvement on the first lot, but they were actually worse: graceless, self-serving, beyond parody.

The expenses-fiddling might have been forgiven, at a pinch, but not this grotesque collective failure to make a satisfactory apology. A scandal that had seemed to be mainly about money became a scandal about the way we communicate with each other in modern Britain, groping for the right words, mangling syntax, aping feelings.

Here is just one of umpteen such apologies, delivered to the House of Commons by Tony McNulty on 29 October 2009. The Labour MP had been officially censured for claiming expenses on the house in which his parents lived, just eight miles from his main home. He duly apologised, but in such a cack-handed way, ineptly mixing his messages, that his political stock fell even further

'. . . I apologise for any part I have played in the diminution of the standing of this House in the eyes of the public. It is, however, time to move on. I apologise once again without reservation, Mr Speaker . . .'

The demand that other people move on, sandwiched tight between the expressions of contrition, makes a mockery of the contrition. The apologiser is making the oldest mistake in the book, pre-empting his own forgiveness. The whole structure of the apology – and this was not an off-the-cuff speech, remember, but a carefully prepared statement – was laughable.

It was also, alas, typical of the age in which it was written. We apologise more and more frequently, but less and less elegantly. We have lost the knack, the way we have lost the knack of tying ties and writing thank-you letters. If a celebrity is snapped on a Barbados beach revealing a square millimetre of cellulite or the first hint of a paunch, they will be held up to public ridicule. If the same celebrity issues a clumsy apology, rotten to the core, a verbal car crash, nobody takes them to task. There is a culture of mediocrity.

Week after week we are subjected to so-called apologies that fail the most basic test: there is no contrition and no acceptance of responsibility. Yet, the kind of pedants who can spot a split infinitive or grocer's apostrophe at a hundred yards wave them through without protest. Newspaper headlines proclaim that so-and-so has said sorry for such-and-such, but as soon as you look at the actual words that so-and-so has used, you realise that you have been the victim of a cynical confidence trick.

I thought Tony McNulty had plumbed the depths of absurdity, but his effort was later trumped during the 2010 Election campaign by the normally sure-footed David Cameron. On 15 April, in the first of the three televised debates between the party leaders, Mr Cameron's opening statement contained the following gem of disingenuousness, a line which he had clearly spent days rehearsing:

'I'm extremely sorry for everything that's happened.'

It *sounds* contrite, but how on earth can one MP take on his shoulders the misconduct of 650 others? If he had said he felt bad about what had happened, that would have been acceptable, albeit banal, but to wheel out the s-word, like a flagellant showing his stripes, and yet accept responsibility for nothing, was cynicism on stilts. It was a textbook case of someone eating humble pie and getting greedy, like a child in a sweet shop.

The Tory leader enjoys apologising, so he said sorry, ticked that box, threw in 'extremely', got bonus points for that, then went for broke with 'everything' – which, once you spot its inherent absurdity, makes a mockery of the whole apology. In fact, it is not an apology at all: it is a pseudo-apology, of the type that is becoming increasingly common.

Anyone who studies the wording of the apology for two seconds can see it is a turkey. But despite its being uttered in front of ten million viewers, in one of the most eagerly awaited television events of 2010, the Tory leader got away with it. His opponents did not demur and there was not a murmur of criticism in the press the next day. The conclusion is inescapable: we just meekly accept sub-standard apologies the way we accept f-words on Channel 4 and English teachers who do not know how to spell.

At least David Cameron was in good company – the highest company of all. You would think that if anyone on the planet could be regarded as an expert in apologising, steeped in the ways of contrition, wise in his understanding of how to confess to wrongdoing and atone for it, it would be His Holiness the Pope. Well, you would think wrong.

In March 2010, after years of prevarication, Pope Benedict XVI issued a lengthy apology to the victims of sexual abuse by Catholic priests in Ireland. The key sentence in his pastoral letter, read out from pulpits across Ireland, ran:

'You have suffered grievously and I am truly sorry.'

Just imagine you are one of the victims of that abuse and having to listen to that weaselly sentence. It is disgraceful. It is like an adulterer saying: 'My wife's crying her eyes out and I am truly sorry.' Or a burglar saying: 'The bank's been robbed and I am truly sorry.' Or a murderer saying: 'There's a dead body on the floor and I'm truly sorry.' The whole sequence of thought is awry. There is a syntactical tricksiness that is rather shocking in a man of God.

The sentence purports to be an apology, but the way it is crafted, quite deliberately, with 'sorry' coming at the end, where it is a waste of space, means it is not an apology at all, just an expression of sympathy. There is a glaring omission of what the situation demanded: an acceptance that the victims suffered at the hands of the Catholic Church, of which the Pope is head. Not surprisingly, the 'apology' did not bring the closure the Vatican wanted, it just made people in Ireland even angrier.

By a nice irony, the Pope received a model apology a few weeks later from a body usually fabled for speaking in forked tongues: the Foreign Office. A leaked document circulating around Whitehall had suggested that the Papal visit to Britain in September 2010 should be marked by the issue of Benedict-branded condoms, and that His Holiness should be invited to open an abortion clinic. The Foreign Office apology was a humdinger – sackcloth and ashes with bells on – probably one of the most unequivocal apologies it has ever issued:

'The Foreign Office very much regrets this incident and is deeply sorry for the offence which it has caused.'

Bullseye! There is not just true remorse, but an acceptance of responsibility, without fudging. A lot of people drafting this kind of apology bail out at the last minute and say sorry for 'any offence that *may* have been caused'. But not the Sir Humphreys at the Foreign Office. In fact, their effort is so superior to the Pope's effort to apologise to the Irish that you wonder whether they should be seconded to the Vatican to give seminars on the subject.

The paradox of the word 'sorry' is that a versatile word, useful in all kinds of different contexts, is also an incredibly hard word to use correctly. It may be versatile, but it is also ambiguous. How often do we want to apologise but become tongue-tied and defensive? We rehearse our lines, but the lines sound wrong, for reasons we find hard to analyse. And if other people are hanging on our words, it only makes the process harder.

We live in a theatrical age. Apologising has become a spectator sport, one of the great English rituals such as afternoon tea or moaning about the national football team. When a public figure screws up, the rest of us hold our breath and wait for them to say sorry, curious as to how they will dig themselves out of the hole.

We want them to make a good job of it and grasp the nettle skilfully. They have hours, days, to get it right, helped by a small army of lawyers and PR advisers, but there is no guarantee that they will get it right, just as there is no guarantee that a Hollywood actress with weeks to choose her outfit for the Oscars ceremony will avoid a fashion *faux pas*.

In fact, they are far more likely to get it wrong than right. Witness those countless celebrity apologies that miss the mark by a country mile. They just sound contrived, like lines in a bad play.

As spectators in the comedy of transgression and reparation, we wait to hear what the miscreants have to say, but more in hope than expectation. We have heard too many sub-standard apologies before. We have become jaundiced about the s-word. The more shrilly we demand the word of others, the more our demands are frustrated. Is it any wonder we have turned into a nation of cynics?

Things have got out of kilter. Our appetite for apologies is undiminished, but we cannot satisfy that appetite. Britain has become a moral quagmire, with the distinction between right and wrong increasingly blurred and even people who know they have done wrong, and want to make amends, unable to express that sentiment in words that other people can accept.

Like a verbal banana skin, the s-word trips up people who are otherwise articulate, even eloquent. In September 2009, Sir Alex Ferguson won plaudits across the football world for his address at the memorial service for his fellow manager Sir Bobby Robson: it was delivered without notes, and there was not a word out of place. But a month later, when Ferguson broke the habit of a lifetime and apologised to a referee he had insulted – Alan Wiley, whom he had accused of being physically unfit after a match at Old Trafford – the garbled language he deployed could have come straight out of the British Airways apology book.

'I apologise to Mr Wiley for any personal embarrassment my remarks may have caused,' he wrote in a message on the Manchester United website. 'In retrospect, I accept that this could be deemed as expressing those views in an inappropriate forum.'

The apology was generally welcomed, if only because of its novelty value. Nobody expected a batsqueak of contrition from a man whose intemperate rants about referees have become legendary, but in cold print the words Ferguson used are awful: a caricature of the corporate apology that is one of the blots on the landscape of twenty-first-century Britain.

If Ferguson sent out a Manchester United team in which more than half the side were carrying injuries, or playing out of position, he would be pilloried on all sides, but these two sentences, word for word, are just as inept. 'Personal embarrassment', 'may have caused', 'in retrospect', 'could be deemed', 'inappropriate'. Anyone with any sort of ear for language would have struck out the phrases after reading the apology in draft. They sound wrong because they are wrong. There is a spinsterish timidity about them, comical in anyone, but, in the mouth of a red-blooded bruiser from Govan, ridiculous.

Ferguson's apology, and the same is true of most apologies made by politicians, was rooted in tactical considerations. There had been an outcry over his comments about the referee and he was facing disciplinary sanctions from the FA; so saying sorry served his own short-term interests. But what is so exasperating about such apologies is how rarely the apologiser seems to grasp the basic point of what he is doing, which is *to show remorse in a convincing way*.

If nobody reading your words of apology believes that you really are sorry, you have failed the most basic test. That is true whether you are an eminent football manager or someone sending a grovelling email to a friend whom you have upset. In which case, and this should be self-evident, you cannot afford the words you choose to be dry, cautious, legalistic and riddled with caveats: they must have the ring of emotional truth.

In October 2009, when Stephen Fry landed himself in hot water after he made comments that appeared to hold the Poles responsible for Auschwitz, he did not pussy-foot about but apologised unstintingly. 'My words were idiotic, ignorant and offensive,' he wrote in his blog. 'What was I thinking? It was a rubbishy, cheap and offensive remark which I have been regretting ever since. I take this opportunity to apologise now. I said a stupid, thoughtless and fatuous thing.' A bit over-the-top? It is a matter of taste, but better Stephen Fry lashing himself like a medieval flagellant than Alex Ferguson mincing his words.

As a strong man, the Manchester United manager should have been strong enough to issue a strongly worded apology. Instead, because strong men hate apologising, he issued a laughably weak apology. And he is not the only one. That same pattern – weak language in a person normally associated with robust language – is repeated again and again.

Listen to Ferguson's fellow Scot/serial blasphemer Gordon Ramsay eating humble pie in 2009 after making offensive remarks about an Australian journalist, Tracy Grimshaw, whom he had likened to a pig, probably lesbian.

'With hindsight,' said a spokesman for the chef (and as soon as you hear the first two words you know this is going to be one of these lickspittle apologies you associate with British Telecom) 'he realises that his comments were inappropriate and offensive.' *Inappropriate?* There is a fatal disconnect between the person and the language used. You can bet that, in his entire professional career, Ramsay has never once told a sous-chef that burning vegetables or letting sauces curdle was inappropriate. It was only the fact of having to apologise that turned him from a plain-talking man into a thesaurus.

He would have been far better off apologising in character. 'Sorry, guys. I behaved like a ****ing idiot. Didn't have my ****ing brain in gear. Out of ****ing order. Can't believe I made such a ****ing ****-up. And I'm ****ing sorry.' Everyone would have had a good laugh and the apology would have been accepted, instead of being treated with derision.

Few people anywhere in the world have achieved such mastery of mass communications as Rupert Murdoch, but in February 2009, when the Australian newspaper mogul was forced to apologise to readers of the *New York Post* after the paper had printed a cartoon seemingly likening Barack Obama to a chimpanzee, the best he could manage was this:

'The buck stops with me. Last week, we made a mistake. We ran a cartoon that offended many people. Today, I want to personally apologise to any reader who felt offended, even insulted.'

It is not the worst apology ever issued: you can catch the tones of the plain-talking Aussie who does not beat about the bush. An Englishman in the same situation would have resorted to timid circumlocution and apologised for 'any offence that might have been caused'. But how on earth can a newspaper owner apologise 'personally' to a million-odd readers, most of whom he has never met and never will? It is a ludicrous choice of word. In fact, the more you think about it, the more ludicrous it gets.

I don't think Murdoch was being deliberately cynical. He just found himself in apology mode and, like so many high-profile apologists, lunged for words that would sound good, rather than ones that would encapsulate what he wanted to say.

So many public figures make so many mangled apologies that, as often as not, the initial controversy they have sparked is followed by a second controversy, as people pick over the words they have used. Was that apology really an apology? Did it sound reasonably sincere or totally contrived? Where was the s-word? On and on they rumble, those tedious semantic arguments, all totally avoidable if the apologiser had used plain English in the first place.

Who can forget Des Browne, Secretary of State for Defence in the last Labour government, giving this deathless reply to a Tory questioner in April 2007? Mr Browne had been forced to apologise to the House of Commons after his department had authorised that Royal Navy personnel who had been captured by the Iranians could sell their memoirs. His apology sounded thin, so there were demands that he beef it up. Mr Browne, nervously, obliged:

'It seems clear to me that I have expressed a degree of regret that can be equated with an apology. If you want me to say "I am sorry", I am happy to say "I am sorry".'

Never can the word 'happy' have been used by a man so patently *un*happy. It was like watching teeth being extracted. But then, that is what the s-word does to some people. The prospect of using it in public fills them with primal terror. It is a taboo word, like 'death', or 'penis', or 'Mandelson'. Why can't they embrace the word; see it as a friend, not an enemy?

I am not arguing for indiscriminate, round-the-clock apologies, either in the House of Commons or anywhere else. If crassly worded apologies are irritating, they are no more irritating than knee-jerk apologies when no apology is called for. We live in a politically correct age when public bodies are terrified of upsetting anyone for any reason. They hoist the white flag at the first sign of trouble. They are afraid to say: 'Well, actually we're *not* sorry, because we haven't done anything wrong. If you choose to take offence, that's your look-out.'

The BBC is particularly culpable. It only takes two nutters and a dog complaining about a programme for the corporation to go into meltdown, rushing out apologies to 'anyone who may have been offended'.

You can bet your life that if I delivered that last sentence on air some nutter would ring in to complain that my use of the word 'nutters' was offensive to people suffering from mental illnesses, gratuitously bracketing them with dogs, and that the BBC would take the side of the nutter, apologising for any offence caused. They would not challenge the nutter to explain the basis for his objections, still less tell him that he was overreacting. They would simply take the line of least resistance, kow-towing to the bullies instead of standing up to them.

Apologies of the sorry-if-we-have-offended-anyone type are not just irritating, but they also have a knock-on effect or, rather, two distinct knock-on effects. On the one hand they embolden the complaining classes to cry foul at the slightest provocation. On the other, they fortify the prejudices of people at the other end of the apologising spectrum: the bullet-heads who think that only wimps say sorry. The result is two competing ideologies of apologising that are at loggerheads with each other.

There was a textbook clash between the two ideologies in February 2009, with Carol Thatcher taking centre stage. Baroness Thatcher's daughter, a roving reporter for *The One Show* on BBC1, had likened a black tennis player to a 'golliwog', one of those grinning dolls that were in vogue when she was a child. It was a private remark, made in the green room, but it leaked out and there was a clamour for Thatcher to apologise, which she did through a spokeswoman:

'Carol Thatcher does not condone any racist comments. It was a private remark, said in jest, and she regrets any inconvenience caused.'

This apology was not good enough to save Thatcher's bacon and she was promptly sacked by the BBC, to the disgust of her fans. Her spokeswoman was sulphurous:

'We issued a proper apology, which they decided was not good enough for them, but it was fulsome enough to us. Who are they to decide what is and isn't a genuine apology?'

There was a good deal of sympathy for Thatcher, sacked for private remarks, and much irritation with the BBC, who had failed to sack other presenters – Jonathan Ross, most notably – who had made far more offensive comments on air. But in one respect at least, the BBC was spot-on. Look at Carol Thatcher's original apology and, in particular, at the phrase 'any inconvenience caused'. It is a woeful choice of words, recklessly euphemistic. Whatever black people who resent being likened to golliwogs feel, it is certainly not inconvenience. The apology sounds like a bad caricature of a Virgin Trains' apology for the fact that the 16.23 from Brighton is ten minutes late. In fact, it barely qualifies as an apology at all: it is just verbal pap, someone who doesn't feel sorry saying they are sorry because someone else has ordered them to apologise. In the clash of wills – between the irresistible force of political correctness and the immovable object of a female called Thatcher – something had to give.

It was an unedifying episode, but hardly an isolated one. That kind of *impasse* has become one of the defining features of our cultural landscape. The British tribe is split down the middle, with one half doffing its collective forelock while the other gives a V-sign of defiance. There is a polarisation in attitudes, with fewer and fewer people prepared to occupy the middle ground and adopt a sensible, pragmatic attitude to apologising.

Which, if you ask me, is a pretty sorry state of affairs.

2

what's in a word?

If one judges words by quantity not quality, and measures their usefulness by the frequency with which people use them, 'sorry' can claim to be one of the most successful words in the history of the English language. Other words come and go, squeezed out by newcomers to the dictionary, but 'sorry' just gets bigger and bigger. It is the Starbucks of apologising; a verbal juggernaut, flattening the opposition. An Englishman without his s-word is an Englishman naked.

You use the word once, then you use it again five minutes later, then again five minutes after that. Even when you hesitate to use it, you think about using it. It is part of the mental landscape of our country – a land where sex is optional but saying sorry is compulsory. If you haven't said sorry at least once before breakfast you feel like a total heel.

It is hardly surprising that simple words such as 'nose' and 'sun' and 'dog', or even abstract terms such as 'good' and 'love' and 'war', have entered the language and, once there, have achieved an unassailable place. Why tinker with them? They do the job they are meant to do. A dog is a dog is a dog. But 'sorry', a word of a different level of complexity altogether, enjoys no such natural monopoly. It has had to fight off synonym after synonym, alternative after alternative, as different generations of Britons have found different ways of apologising. That it should have achieved the status of a classic, a word for all seasons, even though it is a relative newcomer to the language (at least in its modern sense) is extraordinary.

There is only one fly in the ointment: we now use the word far, far too often. It has been coarsened by overuse, like 'nice' and 'jolly' and 'actually', and those other bits of verbal Polyfilla with which the British like to pad out their conversations around the teapot.

I am as guilty of this as anyone, for which I apologise unreservedly. I was recently visiting some friends in Buckinghamshire when I tripped over their golden retriever, who was lying under the table. 'Sorry,' I said, upon instinct – not to my friends, but to the dog, who looked mystified. Her vocabulary doesn't extend beyond 'sit', 'stay' and 'walkies', so I had taken her out of her conversational depth. But still, as of ancient habit, I used the s-word. It seemed the decent thing to do.

If it had been the other way round and the dog had tripped over me, she would have found a far more eloquent way of apologising. No words, just one of those mournful looks of which dogs are past masters and their owners can recognise a mile off. We are supposed to be the more intelligent species, but we are not very good at showing it, spraying s-words around like so much confetti.

In a lifetime of compulsive apologising, I have said sorry not just to dogs, but to cats, horses, pigeons, beggars, dodgy plumbers, traffic wardens, Ryanair check-in staff (Ryanair!) and a girlfriend I caught in bed with another man. 'Sorry,' I said, beating a hasty retreat from the bedroom. The other man looked gobsmacked. I had stolen his line.

A 2007 survey by the insurance company Esure found that the word 'sorry' is used an estimated 368 million times a day in the UK. That is not quite as grim as it sounds. If you discount all the people who never say sorry on principle – bankers, lawyers, politicians, football managers, the Inland Revenue, utility companies, newspaper editors, head teachers, Jeremy Clarkson, bouncers in Soho nightclubs – that leaves the rest of us with a ration of ten s-words a day, a bare minimum if you are a serial adulterer or have to travel on crowded trains in the rush hour. But even so, it is a pretty terrifying statistic, a snapshot of an entire community suffering from the same personality disorder.

The survey, based on interviews with 1,100 people, concluded that the average Briton will say 'sorry' around 1.9 million times in his or her lifetime, which would be interesting, if true. Come on, Esure! Who did your sums for you? Michael Winner? If we only say sorry 368 million times a day between us, we would each have to live for the best part of a millennium to rack up that many s-words. But, with apologies on behalf of Esure for their ropy arithmetic, it is indubitable from their findings that we say sorry to each other indiscriminately, with promiscuous abandon.

The Esure survey also itemised the five most popular reasons for saying sorry, which only underlined how the word has become trivialised through overuse. They were, in order of frequency:

- telling somebody we did not have time to do something ('Sorry, I don't have time to speak right now');
- apologising on behalf of someone else, for example, a misbehaving child or dog ('Sorry, he doesn't usually chew furniture');
- telling someone we did not hear what they said ('Sorry, can you repeat that?');
- asking someone to explain something ('Sorry, I don't quite understand the point you are making');
- and, dismayingly low down the pecking order, apologising for having let someone down, lied to them or otherwise wronged them ('Sorry, darling, I shouldn't have put arsenic in your mother's tea').

The obvious inference – and you only have to listen to everyday conversation to reach the same conclusion – is that 'sorry' for the British has become no more than a verbal tic, mere grouting in the architecture of a sentence, like the ubiquitous 'like' in America ('I wanted to, like, throw up when I saw that there was, like, a cockroach in my salad').

Most of the times the word 'sorry' gets used it has none of the solemnity and resonance of an old-fashioned *mea culpa* – which, paradoxically, makes it harder, not easier, to deploy when you want to make a full-dress apology. There is a temptation to gild the lily ('I'm really, really sorry') rather than speak straight from the heart.

I remember, years ago, having to apologise to a woman whom I had treated badly, *really* badly. Finding the right words was a virtual impossibility; that week alone I had said sorry for coughing, sneezing, interrupting, forgetting to wipe my shoes, spilling coffee on the *Radio Times*, overcooking a £10 rump steak and slagging off Americans, so my bolt was shot. I don't remember exactly what form my apology took, I just remember that the s-word, which should have been the centrepiece, was greeted with derision.

Where did it all go wrong? How did this innocuous-looking word achieve such an unholy grip on our lives?

People of an etymological bent tend to assume that 'sorry' is just an adjectival version of the noun 'sorrow'. In fact, the two words have a separate lineage. 'Sorrow' comes from the archaic word '*sorg*', an Old English noun meaning 'regret' or 'grief', while 'sorry' derives from '*sarig*', an adjective formed from the archaic form of 'sore', in the sense of a source of nagging pain.

In Chaucer, 'sory' is just a jobbing adjective, a linguistic foot soldier, equivalent in meaning to 'pitiful' or 'heartsick'. It is pressed into service when the verse calls for a suitable two-syllable word ('with disconfort and sory countenance'), but achieves little by way of emotional resonance and occurs just thirty-five times in the whole of *The Canterbury Tales*. There is no hint of the protean super-word that is the modern 'sorry'.

Even by the time of the *King James Bible*, published in 1611, the word is still a bit-part player in the English language. There are only four uses of the word in the Old Testament, seven in the New Testament. In meaning, the word has not advanced since Chaucer. In Matthew, 17:23, when Jesus foretells his own death and his disciples are 'exceeding sorry', there are no connotations of guilt or contrition. The s-word simply delineates a state of sadness.

Shakespeare, typically, uses the word with greater elasticity, nudging it in new and unexpected directions. 'This is a sorry sight,' says Macbeth. 'I may do that I shall be sorry for,' says Brutus. 'I am sorry that thou art not well,' Juliet tells the Nurse. But, as an instrument of apology, an admission of wrongdoing, the word is still finding its feet. Probably the closest approximation to an apology in the modern sense comes in *The Tempest*, one of the last plays Shakespeare wrote, when Stephano tells Caliban: 'I am sorry I beat thee.' But elsewhere, particularly in scenes of high emotion, Shakespeare prefers richer, less insipid, language.

When Hamlet apologises to Laertes, he does not use the s-word, but says: 'Give me your pardon, sir. I've done you wrong.' Hamlet being Hamlet, he then rabbits on for another twenty lines, explaining himself *ad nauseam* and making all the textbook mistakes of the apologiser, diluting the apology with excuses, caveats and psychobabble. ('Was't Hamlet wrong'd Laertes? Never Hamlet . . . Who does it, then? His madness.' *Not my fault, Laertes, old man, I suffer from clinical depression. Hamlet really should have been a defence lawyer.*) But the apology itself is immaculate, with the admission of guilt accompanied by a plea for forgiveness.

In Elizabethan times, admitting fault and asking for forgiveness (another lovely recurring phrase in Shakespeare is 'I cry you mercy') were inextricably linked, and that linkage would remain intact for hundreds of years.

It is interesting to fast-forward from *Hamlet* to *David Copperfield*, written two and half centuries later. 'I beg your pardon, sir,' David says to his stepfather, Mr Murdstone. 'I am very sorry for what I did, and I hope you will forgive me.' By this stage Dickens is using the s-word in its modern sense, incorporating notions of contrition that would have been foreign to Chaucer; but the apology is still framed as a request for forgiveness, in a way that most apologies in 2010 are not.

Life for today's apologisers would be a lot simpler if 'I beg your pardon' had retained its popularity as a synonym for 'sorry', instead of being one of those pompous phrases that only Uncle Arthur and Auntie Mildred use. I blame Nancy Mitford, partly. Her famous catalogue of non-U expressions in *Noblesse Oblige* included saying 'Pardon?' when you had not heard what someone had said. The word has been on the skids ever since, leaving 'sorry' so far ahead of the field that it is not worth other words trying to catch up. Indeed, the s-word has taken over the whole apologising show, despite the fact that, at root, it is just the same unprepossessing runt of a word that Chaucer used to pad out his iambic pentameters.

So that is where we are – in a lexicological mess of our own making. It is often claimed that one of the glories of the English language is its flexibility, with new words being coined every day and new uses found for old words, but in the case of 'sorry', which should have been put out to grass years ago, discarded as unfit for purpose, there is no such creative vitality, just sloppy thinking on a cataclysmic scale. Where other words have confined themselves to the use for which they were intended, the s-word has succumbed to middle-aged spread, taking on new functions without ditching old ones.

We can now be sorry about something ('I'm sorry about my snoring'), sorry for something ('I'm sorry for calling you a pillock'), feel sorry for ourselves, feel sorry someone else is feeling sorry for *themselves* ('I'm sorry you feel like that'), conditionally sorry ('I'm sorry if this is starting to sound like gibberish'), or just plain sorry ('Sorry, darling, I forgot to buy marmalade'). We can say sorry *to* someone else ('I would like to say sorry to my wife, my children and, last but not least, my constituents'), make someone sorry, or just have a good old British moan that it is a sorry state of affairs when everyone has to say sorry the whole time.

There is just no stopping a word when it starts to behave like a runaway train. Even now, some spotty teenager in Milton Keynes is probably using 'sorry' as a verb ('I'm going to sorry that bastard'), which will catch on in the playground, which will be adopted by football commentators, and which will eventually find its way into leaders in the *Daily Telegraph*. It would be easier to cage the wind than to stop the s-word proliferating.

If people get the government they deserve, they also get the language they deserve. Different societies over time have evolved different ways of apologising by using forms of words that mirror their cultural values and traditions.

You think the French are a nation of drama queens, gesticulating frantically when a raised eyebrow would do the trick? Then ponder the fact that their favourite way of saying sorry is '*Je suis désolé*', 'I am desolate', which is so over-the-top that it should be wrapped in a *tricoleur* and set to the Marseillaise.

You are puzzled why the Chinese are so obsessed with saving face? Then note that if you want to apologise in Mandarin you have to say '*dui bu qi*', which means roughly, 'I can't raise my face to meet yours'. Saying sorry in China involves real shame: it is not just a form of words.

You think the Italians are spaghetti-eating narcissists? Your prejudices may be confirmed by the fact that a common Italian expression for 'I'm sorry' is '*Mi dispiace*', 'It displeases me'. Not: 'I've hurt your feelings', but 'I've hurt *my* feelings'. What a sad decline from the days of classical Latin when '*mea culpa*' was the simplest, clearest formula for apologising ever invented, unrivalled in its limpidity.

You think the Spanish are barbaric because they kill bulls for fun? Note their equally self-centred way of saying sorry: '*Lo siento*', which translates as 'I feel it'. Feel what? It is a ludicrous cop-out. There are probably ageing Andalusian matadors who murmur '*Lo siento*' as the dead bull is being carted out of the *corrida*. If they had to apologise to the bull, not make a melodrama of their own feelings, they might regain their moral compass.

In much the same way, one of our own national vices – an inability to call a spade a spade – is reflected in our slovenly use of the s-word. In English usage 'I'm sorry' is routinely used in two totally different contexts: as an expression of sympathy ('I'm sorry to hear your aunt has died'); and as an admission of guilt ('I'm sorry I was rude to your aunt'). We are all familiar with both usages, and we all deploy them on a regular basis – they are basic tools of communication in our society. But the scope for confusing the two kinds of 'sorry', with resultant ambiguity, is almost limitless. Only a nation with an aversion to plain talking could have allowed the ambiguity to fester for so long.

What does it say about us as a people that we use exactly the same word to apologise and to *pretend* to apologise? Take that sentence I have just quoted, 'I'm sorry I was rude to your aunt', now just give it a little tweak: 'I'm sorry your aunt was upset by my comments'. The s-word is still there, but the apology has vanished into thin air.

The word is as slippery as an eel. We love to hear it: it induces a slavering, Pavlovian gratitude. If someone has said sorry, everything must be hunky-dory again. But we are hopeless at deconstructing the word, at distinguishing between an apologetic sorry and a non-apologetic sorry. We just lurch from s-word to s-word, like drunks zigzagging along the street.

I remember as a schoolboy being caned by some sour-faced peda-gogue for some misdemeanour. I forget exactly what I had done, I just remember stammering, 'I'm sorry, sir', and the teacher saying, 'You *will* be sorry' as he reached for his cane. My feelings of injustice about the caning were exacerbated by a vague sense that I had been conned. The devious bastard. He had taken my word and twisted it for his own purposes.

In certain contexts, a lack of precision is not altogether a bad thing; in fact, it may explain the remarkable popularity of the s-word. Saying one thing and meaning something different may be a bit sneaky, but it is a form of sneakiness of which we are all guilty. For most people most of the time, all that matters is getting through the day in one piece, without upsetting anyone or getting drawn into acri-monious confrontations. And there is no better prophylactic against such confrontations than the s-word. It is the coward's comforter, the appeaser's friend.

Vagueness is all. Take those asinine public apologies for the slave trade etc. As the apologiser has no personal responsibility for those wrongs, and was not even born when the wrongs were committed, all he is really doing is saying: 'I feel bad about the slave trade.' But if he just said that, everyone would laugh their heads off and wonder why he was making such a song and dance about it. Saying sorry sounds more sonorous.

There is a lot to be said sometimes for making the right sort of noises without being over-precise; and if the s-word helps achieve that, well and good. Take that oft-heard refrain at railway stations: 'We are sorry to announce that the 8.17 from Leamington Spa is running twenty minutes late.' It *sounds* like an apology, but strip it down to its bare bones and it is no more than a polite expression of regret, the equivalent of 'We are sorry it is raining', with no acceptance of liability. However, the ambiguity has its drawbacks. If the 8.17 from Leamington Spa is running late because of heavy fog in Coventry, no apology is needed: the train company is just exercising proper caution. But suppose it is late because the driver of the train has forgotten to set his alarm clock or has slipped out of the station for a quick pint in the Fox and Grapes? Now a grovelling apology is needed, for which the s-word barely feels adequate because it has been used so liberally on other occasions.

A catch-all word is actually a catch-nothing word. There is no clear link between the language used and the feelings behind the language, just a gaping hole into which ambiguities rush.

In March 2000, when disgraced ex-Cabinet minister Jonathan Aitken was interviewed on *Breakfast with Frost*, after serving time in prison for perjury, he made what sounded like an unreserved apology: 'I lied and I am sorry I lied.' Compared with the prevarications of other politicians in similar circumstances, his words had a touching simplicity: he had done wrong, and admitted as much, without excuses. But study his words closely and they reveal their ambiguity. Was Aitken saying: 'I told lies and I apologise for those lies'? Or was he saying: 'I told lies and I wish I hadn't, because I paid a heavy price'? They are different things.

People wanted to hear Aitken say sorry, and were glad when he did, but was he genuinely repentant or just feeling sorry for himself? We couldn't be sure because he didn't have the linguistic tools to tell us; the answer had fallen between the cracks in the language.

*   *   *

Foreigners studying English are completely baffled by the s-word. How can it possibly be right to use the same word in such a wide variety of contexts, apologising in identical terms for offences that are of a different order of seriousness? 'I'm sorry I'm late.' 'I'm sorry I forgot our wedding anniversary.' 'I'm sorry I had a three-month affair with your sister.' Isn't English supposed to have more words than any other language, an Aladdin's cave of slick verbs and sexy epithets?

So, the foreigners scour their dictionaries for alternatives. Perhaps if they didn't say they were sorry they were late, but said they *regretted* they were late . . . No good. Hopeless. 'I regret' is just as ambiguous as 'I'm sorry'. In fact, it is even more ambiguous. On the one hand it hints at contrition without guaranteeing contrition. You can hardly say you regret punching someone in the face: stronger language is needed. On the other it introduces a note of wistfulness that is quite inappropriate if all you are doing is apologising for missing a bus. 'I rue'? Too archaic. 'I repent'? Too Biblical. 'I am guilty'? Sounds like something a shoplifter would say. So it is back to the drawing board and that ugly mongrel of a word, 'sorry': omnipresent, part of the verbal landscape of Britain, but totally untrustworthy.

Children, curiously, use the s-word more proficiently than their parents. I have a friend who is the mother of two small boys, aged five and seven. The boys, like all siblings, fight like alley cats. The mother, like all mothers, plays the peacemaker. I find her even-handedness rather touching. 'Jake, say sorry to Thomas.' 'Thomas, say sorry to Jake.' Those same two lines, again and again, alternating like clockwork. Sometimes the s-word is slow in coming – Jake, I have noticed, is more allergic to the word than his brother – but as soon as it is produced, there is closure. 'Sorry, Thomas.' 'Sorry, Jake.' Then harmony rules again. If only adults could apologise so cleanly, without cluttering up the s-word with other words, diluting its impact. But that is not the adult way. We live in terror of simplicity.

A lot of sorry-sayers, conscious of the ambiguities of the s-word, prefer the more formal 'I apologise', or variants thereof. But even here the English language is fatally imprecise. 'I apologise' passes muster in written apologies, but in spoken apologies it tends to sound vaguely pompous, betraying its Greek origins.

The word 'apology' only emerged in its modern usage in around 1700. It had previously denoted a formal, quasi-legal defence – as in the *Apologia* of Plato – and was not used to signify contrition. But 'apology' rapidly grew into the more nebulous 'apologies', like '*scusi*' in Italian, as if a single apology was not quite enough. The word has never quite bedded down into the language.

Consider the delicious vagueness of that perennial favourite of grovellers, 'I owe you an apology'. The phrase always has a fine theatrical ring: it is the sort of thing Sir Donald Sinden would say in a Restoration comedy. But since when was owing something the same as giving it? I owe Barclaycard £93.72 and have no intention of paying it until the end of the month.

How much do such semantic ambiguities matter? It depends, ultimately, on which side of the apology fence you are standing. If you are the person grovelling, a little wriggle room can be tactically invaluable: you can eat humble pie, but not such a mouthful of humble pie that you start worrying if you have overdone it. If you are the person being grovelled to, the ambiguities can be infuriating. You find yourself waking up at three in the morning and thinking: 'Now was that a genuine apology or was I being taken for a ride?'

In defence of the mongrel s-word, one could point out that there are millions of times every day when it does the trick: makes peace between A and B without blame having to be apportioned too exactly. To that extent, it is a force for good. One could even, without wild exaggeration, link the British passion for saying sorry with another great national characteristic: our genius for mucking along with each other, in a spirit of tolerance, while other countries have revolutions, start wars, become socially fragmented. But in 2010 that would be pretty disingenuous.

Just think how often the s-word, far from making peace, causes fresh division, as people bicker about whether so-and-so is genuinely sorry, or treat an apology as an admission of guilt and therefore demand compensation.

Language, ultimately, happens on the surface. It externalises what we are feeling, but only with 90 per cent accuracy, and sometimes much less than that. When language fails us, it is partly for cultural reasons – our tribe uses a verbal currency that buckles under pressure, like the pound or the euro; and partly for personal reasons – we are clumsy at expressing ourselves.

In order to get to grips with the s-word and be able to use it more effectively ourselves, we need to look at the emotions that give rise to the word.

It is time to talk about contrition.

3

i confess

In the Catholic boarding school I attended in the early 1970s, there was a chapel boys were expected to visit once a week, for the purpose of making their confessions. There were two confessionals, side by side, and two regular father confessors: one tall and thin, the other short and fat. I have forgotten their names; they must both be dead by now. I shall call them Father Edmund and Father Jasper.

As boys filed into the chapel and queued outside the confessionals, a fly on the stained-glass window could not have failed to notice a striking discrepancy: the number of boys queuing to confess their sins to Father Jasper was at least double the number queuing to confess to Father Edmund. If they had been rival sandwich bars you would have concluded that Father Jasper made better sandwiches.

The explanation for the discrepancy was simple enough: Father Edmund, the younger of the two, had excellent hearing; Father Jasper, past seventy, was almost totally deaf. Your sins were safe with him because he could not hear what your sins were. He would just listen to your confession, nodding like an old horse, and absolve you. There was none of the rigorous cross-examination ('So, when you say you have been suffering temptations of the flesh . . .') for which Father Edmund, who should have been a QC, was renowned.

Schoolboys being schoolboys, a visit to Father Jasper's confessional became a party game, with the winner being the boy who could confess to the most outlandish crime (murdering the geography master was popular) and be absolved for it. I never took the mickey out of Father Jasper myself, I was much too timid, but I confess I was tempted.

It all seems slightly surreal now, but the confessional, and the etiquette of the confessional, was an education in itself. It instilled habits of thought that have never left me.

The bottom line in the confessional, whether Father Jasper could hear what you were saying or not, was contrition. If you were truly contrite, you could be forgiven and receive absolution, with Father Jasper acting as a conduit for the mercy of God. No contrition, no absolution. It was as simple as that. Father Jasper might *pronounce* absolution, but if you were trying to pull the wool over his eyes, or had omitted to mention that you had been stealing altar wine or skiving off double maths, the absolution was null and void, like a cheque that had bounced.

It was no good, and this was hardly theological rocket science, merely to make suitably contrite noises; you had to be contrite, otherwise there could be no absolution, whatever Father Jasper said. God would know the truth, so your emotional sincerity was being tested – which, in the great confessional of life, was no bad thing.

Probably the hardest part of confessing was making what was known in the trade as a 'firm purpose of amendment'. Contrition for the past was not good enough: you had to resolve to do better next time and make a genuine effort not to commit the same sins again. It was no good confessing to being beastly to Addington Minor, then going straight back to the playground and giving Addington Minor a sly kick on the shin. No purpose of amendment, no absolution. That was the deal.

There is a lot of that kind of small print in Roman Catholicism, which is what puts some people off the religion. Suppose you are a woman on the Pill, which in Catholic doctrine is sinful, but not very sinful – somewhere between swearing at a traffic warden and shoplifting in Harvey Nichols. You cannot confess to that sin and get absolution unless you intend to come off the Pill, adopt the rhythm method, abstain from sex or become a mother of nine. It's a bummer, isn't it? But, in truth, Catholic doctrines of penance, contrition and forgiveness are rooted in common sense; simple moral precepts that hold good for people of any religion or none.

If I had been raised a Jew, I might not have had Father Jasper to contend with but I would have had to examine my conscience scrupulously prior to Yom Kippur, the annual day of atonement. My feelings, and the truth of those feelings, would have been challenged. Was I *really* sorry? Or was I just saying the word? And did I sincerely intend to mend my ways?

A promise to do better next time is integral to any apology. Take that staple of marriages the world over: 'Darling, I'm really sorry. It was just a drunken one-night stand. It won't happen again.' Deliver the line with conviction, and accompany it with a suitably lavish bouquet of flowers, and you may get away with your peccadillo – once. But the key thing is that you mean what you say. If you intend such drunken one-night stands to become habitual, the sorry-saying is not just hollow, but hypocritical. Nothing kills an apology quicker than insincerity.

I know a fellow writer – probably a lovely man underneath – with one of the worst tempers on the planet. He only has to be kept waiting ten minutes, or be served overcooked vegetables, or be made to listen to a speech by Harriet Harman, or see a penalty awarded against his beloved Chelsea, to go off like an Icelandic volcano. 'Sorr-ee!' he will chirp, five minutes later, as the plaster is still falling from the ceiling.

He accompanies his apologies with a sheepish grin, which he has spent years perfecting. The show of penitence would be rather charming – if you did not know that the next eruption is just around the corner.

This, of course, is where our promiscuous use of the s-word catches us out. We have become so accustomed to saying sorry for minor infringements, like forgetting to pass the salt, that the word trips off our tongue in situations of much greater moral peril. We rush out our apology the moment we are caught transgressing – which casts inevitable doubt on its sincerity.

If you apologise, you should be prepared to accept responsibility for whatever you have done wrong – that is just common sense – but how many apologies pass that rudimentary test?

Here is a particularly fatuous apology from BT that plopped on to my doormat earlier this year. There had been a cock-up with the Oxford telephone directory. These things happen. Tens of thousands of names had been left out of the directory in error, which required a second, supplementary directory to be printed. I have no problem with that. It is an Englishman's birthright to make the occasional cock-up without being pilloried for it. But the wording of the apology was so ridiculous that I couldn't stop giggling.

'The Phone Book from BT apologises for any inconvenience this may have caused.'

How in the name of sanity can a book say sorry? Have printed pages suddenly acquired the power of speech? Couldn't whoever was responsible for the cock-up just have held up his/her hand?

Our indolent use of the s-word has had side effects that go beyond semantics, though. In recent times there have been some quite ludicrously worded apologies by the great and the good (I shall have fun anatomising some of them later in the book), but the inept wording of the apologies is only a small part of the story. *Why* are so many public apologies so ineptly worded? It is not because the apologisers are bad with words, though many are, but because they are not properly contrite. They do not think they have done anything wrong. They feel no remorse. They are just going through the motions.

As they come under fire, and the clamour for them to apologise mounts, all they are thinking about is the choreography. Should they put out a press statement? And when? In time for the lunchtime news, or later in the day? Apologise on camera or do it through a spokesman? Do their grovelling dressed in black or a quiet grey pinstripe? With or without their partner standing loyally by their side? They do not have time to do the necessary soul-searching, or they tell themselves they do not have time, which is not the same thing.

The more successful people are, the more reluctant they are to apologise, which is perhaps not surprising. Behind most successful careers there is an element of ruthlessness, a disinclination to worry about upsetting other people. So when such people are put on the spot and expected to grovel, image, not substance, is the name of the game. *Will an apology make me look better or worse than a refusal to apologise?* That is the riddle they ponder, not the much tougher riddle: *Have I behaved like a total shit?*

Often, the only reason public figures say sorry is that it is expedient for them to do so. Perhaps there is a general election pending. Or perhaps they are due to appear on *Friday Night with Jonathan Ross*. Or perhaps they *are* Jonathan Ross. Or perhaps their PR advisers have warned that if they do not apologise they will lose a lucrative sponsorship deal. Money does wonders for the apology industry.

However, money also coarsens the apology industry, the way it coarsens everything else. It introduces an element of calculation into a process that should be simple, artless and emotionally raw.

Those of us lucky enough to lead our lives out of the public spotlight do not have to make such base calculations, but, when it comes to apologising, we still need to look ourselves in the mirror and confront our own failings. An apology is not a gesture, a verbal mannerism: it must come from the heart.

Like the quality of mercy, the quality of penitence is not strained. If someone is twisting the apologiser's arm, the apology is worthless.

Here is a small example of what I am talking about, a little vignette I observed in The Parks in Oxford this summer. There was a light drizzle, so a middle-class English family was doing what middle-class English families do in light drizzle – playing cricket.

Mum was stationed at extra cover, smiling bravely. Dad was at square leg. He had steel-rimmed glasses and a Heinrich Himmler haircut and I took an instant dislike to him. A girl of about ten was batting, her younger brother was bowling, and a third boy was keeping wicket, crouching behind a rucksack.

'*Howzattt!*' chorused the boys, as the girl took a swipe, missed, and was hit on the knee. Not out, was my immediate reaction. The ball had pitched outside leg stump and was going over the rucksack. Himmler had other ideas. '*Out!*' he yodelled, raising his finger. I suspect he was in a hurry to get to the pub. The girl threw down the bat and stormed off. Not very ladylike, but you had to see it from her point of view: nobody likes being given out LBW by square-leg umpires. Cue the following exchange, twenty-first-century Britain in absurd miniature.

Himmler: Jessica! Say you're sorry to Harry.

Jessica (*stamping her foot*): But Daddy, it wasn't *out*.

Himmler (*chasing after her and grabbing her by the shoulders*): SAY SORRY!

Jessica (*barely audible*): Sorry, Harry.

Himmler (*the colour of a cricket ball*): SAY SORRY PROPERLY!

Jessica: I'm very sorry, Harry.

Mum: Would anybody like an ice cream?

Was it just me, or were there echoes of Prime Minister's Question Time in the clamour for an apology that, although eventually extracted, was null and void? Saying sorry is not like that: an apology must come from within.

In some situations – for example, if you have bumped into someone in the street – saying sorry is just an instinctive, spur-of-the-moment thing. Out the word rushes, like a cough or sneeze: it is almost as if you have no control over your own reflexes. But in more emotionally charged situations, when you have hurt someone you love or had a blazing row with a work colleague, apologising does not have that effortless simplicity. It must begin with a period of honest introspection.

What exactly have you done wrong? How could you have managed things better? Why have you got yourself into this mess? *When* did you get yourself into this mess? The other person is upset, that is obvious – they are crying, shouting, throwing things at you – but are they just upset because they are thin-skinned, or because you have behaved badly, without proper consideration of their feelings?

Examining your conscience is harder than it sounds, which is why it takes a little time. The waters are often muddied by the fact that, although you owe the other person an apology, the other person also owes you an apology; there has been fault on both sides, so the instinct to grovel and the instinct to blame jostle for supremacy in your head. There is an underlying battle of wills, which can become so distracting that it deflects you from your main objective: to be honest with yourself, however painful or embarrassing your findings. Which of us can look at ourselves in the mirror without flinching?

Self-righteousness creeps up on us as we get older. When we are children, we are naughty because all children are naughty. When we are teenagers, we are impossible because all teenagers are impossible. In our twenties, we make mistakes, go off the rails, screw up relationships, act unreasonably and hysterically, because that it is what our twenties are for. But by the time we are in our thirties, we enter a kind of moral comfort zone where we know that, whatever happens, we are not going to end up in a police cell. Our misdemeanours are so petty – a swear word here, a parking ticket there – that we lose the habit of self-criticism altogether. That is a dangerous place to be in.

I know one woman in her early fifties who, to the best of my knowledge, has not apologised for anything since 1993, when she had her collar felt by the Inland Revenue. The older she gets, the more smug she gets – to the point where if she murdered her mother she wouldn't think she had done anything wrong. She has retired from saying sorry, the way some people retire from sex. All very sad; I liked her better in her apologising days.

So you need, first and foremost, to be open to the possibility that, even though you have been taught the difference between right and wrong, you have done wrong, not by accident, or because you were drunk, but by *deliberate choice*. That can be an incredibly hard thing to accept.

People are more comfortable as victims than villains: they like to see themselves as playthings of Fate, not agents of their own downfall. So they shrink from the truth. The naughty step is packed with people who are there because they have been put there, not because they have accepted that it is where they belong. But until you have acknowledged the fact of your wrong-doing, you have not taken the first step on the road to contrition. You are still in denial.

Being honest with yourself can be particularly hard at times of high stress, when the shit has hit the fan and everyone is diving for cover. Emotions take over completely, and you stop looking at things straight. A fly on the wall would be able to look at the situation dispassionately and see where the fault lay, but in the heat of battle, objectivity gets lost. You want to do the decent thing, and take the blame if necessary, but there is no simple correlation between the hurt you have caused and your own culpability.

Say you are a woman who has decided to dump your boyfriend of eighteen months. He adores you. He buys you flowers. He says you look like Jennifer Lopez in your Nicole Farhi jeans. Now he is devastated by your decision. Tears are streaming down his face. He is making desperate promises to give up drinking, do more of the housework, watch less football on television. But does any of that make you a bad person? Or mean that you are wrong to dump him? Love is not compulsory. Relationships are not life sentences. If you no longer love the man, you would be mad to stay with him. You may find yourself saying sorry again and again, as a guilty reflex, but you have nothing to apologise for.

In another type of situation, you may be at fault, and know you are at fault, but get off scot-free. Perhaps the press is unexpectedly kind to you, being distracted by other stories. Or perhaps you are blessed with a generous partner who, after a domestic row, takes all the blame themselves, absolving you of the need to apologise. Now you should say sorry, because honesty and humility require it.

If you simply gauge your need to apologise by taking the emotional temperature, regardless of the facts, you will come unstuck. You need to maintain a moral compass and *trust* that moral compass.

In the majority of situations where A has put B's nose out of joint, there has been no malice involved, just a failure of imagination. A has not thought things through properly; he has not put himself in B's shoes and imagined how B will react in a given situation. That is hardly a hanging offence. Which of us is capable of perfect empathy with another human being? But it is an offence that needs to be identified and acknowledged. A has to travel back in time to the point where he went off the rails, which is harder than it sounds. How many of us have had a row with a loved one and thought, 'I wish to God I had a tape-recording of that conversation we had in the pub last Thursday'? We know we have missed a trick, but not which trick. The devil is in the detail.

A few years back, I had a row with some dear friends of more than twenty years. I knew I was in the doghouse and, in very vague terms, why I was in the doghouse, but relations between us remained cool and my peace overtures fell on deaf ears. It was only by examining the events of the previous month with the precision of a forensic pathologist that I hit on the truth. 'Ah-*ha*!' I thought, as the penny finally dropped. '*That's* why they were giving me such filthy looks in the Chinese restaurant.' A short phone call of apology and everything was hunky-dory again. The slate had been wiped clean.

Most of us lead such hectic lives that, when we have had a row with someone, there is an easy get-out. 'Oh, come on, Paul/Alison/ Michael. Let's not sweat the small stuff. Fault on both sides, yes? Time to move on.' But that is an awfully lazy approach, rooted in self-centred priorities. There is nothing more depressing than people who are happy to spend five hours a week in the gym, listening to dreary ditties on their iPods, but are unable to find five minutes to resolve differences amicably.

You will never master the art of apologising unless you put a little time and effort into it. And it is the first five minutes, when you examine your conscience, see your faults, and *name* those faults, that are the most important.

4

back to basics

So you have got to first base. You have done something wrong, you feel wretched, you have examined your conscience, and now you want to confess – whether to your husband, your boss, your teammates, your constituents, the American people, or the passengers stranded at Luton airport at three in the morning – that you are at fault. What next?

The first, and most important, thing to do is to commit to the apology. If you think to yourself, 'Well, I suppose I'd better say sorry, but I don't want to overdo it', you will be doomed to fail, because that is not how apologies work. You will end up dropping the olive branch like a relay runner dropping the baton. You have to go through with the emotional process you have started, without backtracking or dithering, showing the steely determination of a soldier going into battle. This is no time for half-measures.

Think a move ahead. When you have made your apology, what do you want to see on the face of the other person? A smile of gratitude, or a look of hesitation, as if they are not quite sure whether to accept your apology?

Half-hearted apologies are worse than no apology at all. If you doubt that, you should ponder the findings of a fascinating research study at the University of Illinois in 2006.

Participants in the study were asked to imagine that they had been the victims of a pedestrian – cyclist accident and had received a letter from the other party offering compensation. Where the offer of compensation was accompanied by a full apology, 73 per cent of plaintiffs were prepared to accept the offer – a figure that fell to 52 per cent when no apology was tendered. So far, so predictable; you would expect an apology to have that effect. But it was the third hypothetical scenario that was most revealing.

When a *partial* apology was offered, a mere 35 per cent of plaintiffs were prepared to accept it. In other words, they found ambivalence even less attractive than a complete lack of contrition. So you should avoid that trap at all costs.

The next thing, obvious when you think about it but not always obvious at the time, is to acknowledge the difficulty of what you are attempting. Simply blurting out 'I'm sorry', however contrite you feel, will rarely do the trick; the s-word, as we have seen, is lethally ambiguous, which means that the recipient of your apology is going to want to resolve those ambiguities. If you think you can just say 'I'm sorry', heave a sigh of relief, then lie back like a dog waiting to be tickled, you are in for a shock. Back they will come, like tracer bullets, those probing supplementaries. 'So why did you do it then?' 'How can I be sure you mean it?' 'What's the point of saying sorry if you're just going do the same thing again?'

The s-word is only meaningful if it is part of a larger edifice, but as soon as you start constructing that edifice, you run into semantic difficulties. Even people who are happy to apologise say sorry in such different ways that they could be talking a different language.

The comedy of the sexes would not be complete without misunderstandings about the s-word. In every master bedroom in every marital home in the country, the following conversation, with minor variations, must have taken place a thousand times:

Husband: Sorry, darling.

Wife: But why—

Husband: Didn't stop to think. Sorry.

Wife: You must have known—

Husband: I did. Sorry. Forgot to take that into account.

Wife: But I don't understand—

Husband: Sorry. My fault. I'm not explaining myself very well. Won't do it again.

Wife: Haven't we had this conversation before?

Husband: Probably. Sorry. Well, good night, darling.

Wife: Good night.

The man has said sorry five times, riches indeed, but he hasn't followed through properly. He has just used the s-word to keep his wife sweet. Look, he even strokes her bottom every time he uses the word, to show that he means it. They will probably stay married another thirty years, but it is hard, as a fly on the wall, to withhold a sigh of exasperation. Apologising should be more copious, more generous, more expansive.

Things are not much better if the roles are reversed, with the wife in the doghouse and the husband occupying the moral high ground. Here, the conversation might go something like this:

Wife: Darling, I'm so, so sorry.

Husband: You shouldn't—

Wife: But I feel *awful*. (*Sobs uncontrollably for five minutes.*)

Husband: Why did you do it?

Wife (*brightening*): I've asked myself that again and again. Believe me, darling, I've tried so hard to make sense of what I did. I think things first started going wrong back in 1998. You remember we went to stay with your mother, just after the operation,

45

and Billy was being stroppy, because I'd told him off in front of
Ben, and your mother said . . . (*Continues in the same vein for the
next half hour.*)
Husband (*ageing visibly*): Darling, could we talk about this another
time? The footie's about to start.

Again, the couple will probably stay married another thirty years,
but it is hard to give them more than 5 out of 10 for communication skills. The apology has been turned into grand opera, with the
penitent in the starring role and the needs of the other person largely
ignored.

A good apology is both very simple, straight from the heart, and
very, very complicated, in the sense that it has to serve a number of
distinct purposes at the same time. As a bare minimum (and this list
increases exponentially if you are an American president who has
been fooling around with an intern in the Oval Office) you have to
admit that you are in the wrong, acknowledge that you have hurt
another person in a way that was avoidable, explain how you came to
do what you did, and convince the other person that you will mend
your ways in the future. That is a lot of boxes to tick, and you can see
why so many people cannot be bothered to make the effort, but bury
their heads in the sand and hope for the best.

In terms of complexity, you might liken apologising to one of
those TV cookery shows in which contestants are given a lamb chop,
a clove of garlic, two red onions, a packet of basmati rice, some extra
virgin olive oil, half a pound of mushrooms and a bag of carrots and
have twenty minutes to produce a dish that is presentable and edible.

The different ingredients need to be blended in the right proportion, not just thrown into a pot together, and the clock is ticking. It is
no good producing a perfectly crafted apology if it takes you so long
that by the time your masterpiece is complete your wife has left you

or your constituents have voted for someone else. There is an innate urgency to the process.

But the urgency is no excuse for rushing. If you just come out with a tsunami of s-words ('Darling, I'm so *sorry*, I don't what came over me, I was tired, she's just a friend, honestly, I love you so *much*, let's go to Paris, things are so hectic at work right now, you can't *imagine* how bad I feel, I would *never* deliberately hurt you, it would *never* have happened if . . .'), you will only make the situation worse. Far better to stop, think, compose yourself and give thought to *the exact words you are going to use*.

That may sound as if it runs counter to the first principle of apologising, which is that an apology must come from the heart – and if you get a highly paid lawyer to draft your apology, rather than drafting it yourself, you will get it wrong every time. But it is actually just common sense: If you want to say something really important – make a proposal of marriage, say – you naturally rehearse your lines first. That is not being uptight and unspontaneous: it is showing proper respect for the seriousness of the process.

In the case of an apology, it is important not just to choose your words well, but to structure your apology properly, not just chuck in the different elements at random. Depending on the circumstances, you will probably have some explaining to do. *Why* did you lie to the Inland Revenue, turn up two hours late to the cinema, break a manifesto promise, make a tasteless joke about your mother-in-law? But if you simply rush out the s-word, then launch into a long-winded explanation, you will sound as if you are making excuses – one of the cardinal sins of apologising. Your contrition, assuming it is genuine, will get drowned under an avalanche of detail about bank statements and train timetables. There needs to be a balance between the factual content of an apology – the explanation – and the emotional content – your remorse.

There are few hard-and-fast rules, because the context of each apology is so different, but if you focus on the recipient of the apology, the person whose feelings you have hurt, you will not go far wrong. It is because you have ignored those feelings, or taken them insufficiently into account, that you have got into hot water in the first place. Now you need to redress the balance by treating those feelings – not your own wounded *amour-propre* at finding yourself in the doghouse – as paramount.

This should be obvious, but it is extraordinary how many apologisers fail to grasp the principle, instead fixating on a self-centred, self-justifying agenda. They want to be heroes of their own narrative, which, if they have just done something un-heroic and stupid, is futile.

Here is a small personal example to illustrate the point. A couple of years ago I was due to meet a woman, an editor for whom I hoped to write, for the first time. We agreed to meet in a pub at half-past seven. Unfortunately, through a freak combination of circumstances, with British Rail being the main culprit and others playing a contributory role, I was forty minutes late. Now, everyone who knows me knows that I am normally punctual to a fault – meticulously punctual, fanatically punctual, so punctual you could set your watch by me. So what did I do when I turned up forty minutes late in the pub, puffing and panting? Spend five minutes giving a blow-by-blow account of the malign actions of British Rail and their accomplices, then *another* five minutes explaining how out of character my behaviour was, and how my friends would hardly credit that I had been forty minutes late for an appointment, because I was normally super-punctual, on account of my Swiss mother, and how, in 1997 . . . I could see the woman looking at me with glazed eyes, bored stiff with my maunderings. It was ten minutes before I did what I should have done within seconds of my arrival – offered to replenish her vodka and tonic.

You could say that what I did was human enough. When we have let someone down, for whatever reason, we want to reassure them that our behaviour was an aberration, not the kind of thing we normally do. But my self-justifying apology was also the height of discourtesy. My focus should have been the woman I had kept waiting, the inconvenience I had put her to, and her empty glass.

I have made the same mistake in other situations when more than a vodka and tonic was at stake. It is an easy mistake to make. But that does not make it any less irritating for the other person. A good apologiser should be first and foremost humble, subordinating his own interests to those of the person who really matters – the recipient of the apology.

When Mike Tyson notoriously bit Evander Holyfield's ear in a world heavyweight title fight in Las Vegas, in 1997, his subsequent apology read like an Oscars acceptance speech: 'I apologise to the world, to my family, to the Nevada State Athletic Commission . . . to Judge Patricia Gifford . . . to MGM, to Don King, my promoter, to my team, to the wonderful city of Las Vegas . . .' It was only much later in the statement – so late it sounded like an afterthought – that he got around to saying sorry to the man whose ear he had bitten. More than ten years would pass before the two boxers finally made it up with each other.

Most of us have never done anything so *outré* as biting Evander Holyfield, but exactly the same human dynamics apply in more humdrum situations. The apologiser must take a back seat. He is centre stage *de facto* because he has screwed up. People are hanging on his words, but he must not let the limelight go to his head. He is playing a supporting role.

When saying sorry to someone you have upset, always keep your eyes on the main prize – the smile of gratitude you will get from the other person when you have put right the hurt you have caused.

Think of yourself as a nurse dressing a wound, not a pathologist trying to determine the cause of the wound. Deal with those hurt feelings first. All the messy stuff – the rights and wrongs of a row, who started it, who said what when – can wait for another day. In fact, nine times out of ten, the messy stuff will be forgotten in the rush of relief that normal relations have been restored. People *need* reconciliation, the way they need food and water. Only idiots and Martin Amis get a kick out of twenty-year feuds.

It helps, obviously, when the person to whom you are apologising is someone you know and, better still, when they are in the same room as you – their hurt feelings are so raw you can hardly miss them. But the same principle applies if there is no physical connection between the person giving offence and the person taking offence.

Suppose you are a politician at Westminster who has caused uproar in Newcastle with an insulting reference to Geordies, belittling their intelligence/work rate/dress sense/sexual ethics. You know you have upset people, but you do not know the individual people you have upset: their anger might be venting itself in calls to local radio stations. But before you apologise to them you need to understand their feelings: identify with them imaginatively in their outrage. If you just put yourself centre stage, explain that your comments were completely out of character, or were only meant light-heartedly, or were no worse than something a Liberal Democrat MP said in 1995, you will never salve their hurt. You will just come across as another out-of-touch politician.

A lot of people in the public eye rush out apologies of the 'I'm sorry for any offence caused' variety before they have even acknowledged that the offence is real, not an abstraction. The apologies are next to useless as a result. It is better, before apologising, to spend a few minutes trying to get inside the heads of the people who have taken offence – which may call for some lateral thinking.

Take that stock scenario, many times repeated. White middle-class English person unwittingly makes a remark deemed racially offensive (think Carol Thatcher and 'golliwog'). The person making the remark is told they have caused offence to black people but, because they have never felt racially offended themselves, perhaps because they are part of a secure majority rather than an insecure minority, they cannot fathom what all the fuss is about. They need to remember times when they felt offended for *other* reasons – perhaps by someone being gratuitously rude about redheads, or fat people, or upper-class twits – to connect with the people they have offended.

In the hurly-burly of life we have all had our noses put out of joint; we all know what it is like to feel belittled, taken for granted, insulted, subjected to casual abuse. Equally, we all know how good it feels to be valued again, to be told that our feelings *do* matter, to be on the receiving end of a little TLC from the person who put our noses out of joint in the first place. When the boot is on the other foot, and we are the ones who need to dispense the TLC, we should not hold back. An apology should not be a chore, but a gift.

Should you deliver that gift face-to-face or in writing? Again, that depends on the context, but you should certainly take time to weigh up the pros and cons of the different options available. The art of saying sorry, like the art of cookery, is part substance, part presentation.

There is a lot to be said for a written apology in some situations. For one thing, you can polish and polish until you get the wording right. For another, you can underscore the sincerity of what you want to say by committing it to paper. A half-baked spoken apology can be disowned later, like a fumbled kiss; a written one is set in stone.

When speed is of the essence, an emailed apology is acceptable, at a pinch, though *not* a text message. I still bear the scars of a texted apology I once received which ran as follows: 'V sry Max. U will h8 me, but have to cancel cos work sh*t, lol.' But, in more serious situations, a handwritten letter is preferable. It takes more physical effort than an email, a fact that will be duly noted by the person to whom you are apologising, thus earning you your first Brownie point. As you will need to get a minimum of six Brownie points to be forgiven – more if you are Jonathan Ross or an MP fiddling their expenses – the sooner you start racking them up, the better.

Letter writing is becoming a thing of the past, of course, but the corollary of that is that when you do get a handwritten letter you appreciate it that much more. There are exceptions that prove the rule, however. Poor Gordon Brown, acting from the best of motives, outraged Jacqui Janes, the mother of a soldier killed in Afghanistan in 2009, by sending her a handwritten letter of condolence addressed to Mrs James, not Mrs Janes – a tiny slip which had disastrous consequences. But, by and large, putting pen to paper is a courtesy for which the recipient will thank you.

I still treasure a handwritten letter of apology I once received from a well-known newspaper columnist. 'Max, I'm so sorry,' it began, and continued in the same vein, paragraph after paragraph of remorse, for two pages. It was a bravura performance, the *War and Peace* of grovelling, and it did the trick. An email could never have had the same impact.

Nineteenth-century literature is full of letters of apology, most of them written in a comically orotund style. Take this indigestible mouthful in a letter from that prize creep, Mr Collins, in *Pride and Prejudice*:

'I cannot be otherwise than concerned at being the means of injuring your amiable daughters, and beg leave to apologise for it, as well as to assure you of my readiness to make every possible amends.'

Here the epistolary apology teeters on the brink of self-parody, but the point about letter-writers in nineteenth-century novels is that their missives invariably reach their intended recipients – apart from poor Tess of the D'Urbervilles, whose letter to her husband-to-be gets stuck under the carpet. There is no such certainty with the Royal Mail or, for that matter, with emails. I sent an operatic email of apology last year, but, from the deafening silence at the other end, have never been 100 per cent sure that my bleatings made it through cyberspace.

That element of uncertainty bedevils all written apologies, particularly important ones. Would you entrust a proposal of marriage to postmen who might be drunk, on strike or playing football with the mail bags?

The other big drawback of written apologies, often overlooked, is that you cannot see for yourself how your apology has been received by the other person. Has it done the trick? Or will further fence-mending be needed? There will be an awkward hiatus, which can be avoided if you bite the bullet and take the one unimpeachable, fail-safe option – make your apology in person.

It will not be a comfortable experience, and the outcome will not be a foregone conclusion, but it should be a relatively swift process. The finish line is in sight.

Of course, if you need to apologise to lots of people – everyone in your office, say, or gays in general, or women in general, or two hundred million Americans – apologising in person becomes problematic. But the general principle still holds good: you have upset real people, so you have to mollify those people, which cannot be done if you treat them as theoretical abstractions. Put yourself in their shoes for a minute. What are they hoping for from you? Contrition, obviously, but genuine contrition, the kind they can trust.

If all you give them is words on a page, particularly words that look as if they have been drafted by someone else, they will find it impossible to judge whether your contrition is genuine or not. They want to *see* you – even if they are not able, for logistical reasons, to look you directly in the eye. So you should give them that opportunity, even if means facing a battery of TV cameras, rather than apologising through an intermediary. A press statement is not an apology, and never can be. It is just an exercise in face-saving.

Once you have got the choreography clear in your head – focused on the recipient of the apology and the form of apology that is most likely to meet their needs – you need to turn your attentions to the final piece of the jigsaw, the one that often gets overlooked in the emotional mayhem. For what, precisely, are you saying sorry? Only you know the answer to that question, but unless you have the answer clear in your head, your apology will unravel.

Suppose you have had a blazing row with your wife and, like a friend of mine, have been called 'a pompous, self-centred control freak who treats his children like Victorian servants'. That is four distinct charges: (1) pomposity; (2) selfishness; (3) an over-controlling personality; and (4) cavalier treatment of your children. It is no good just backing down, saying 'I'm very sorry, darling' and trying to make peace that way. My friend made that mistake and promptly got another earful. Further misdemeanours, dating back to 1993, were added to the charge sheet. You need to consider the separate allegations and, if you are prepared to apologise, do so in specific terms. 'You're right, darling. I *am* pompous. I *am* a control freak.' You don't have to apologise for everything you are accused of, not if you think the accusations are unfair, but you do need to hone your apology, rather than confine it to generalities.

Think of yourself as being in a court of law, facing specific charges. You have to plead guilty or not guilty to each charge separately. It may also be possible to plead guilty to a lesser charge – manslaughter rather than murder, careless driving rather than dangerous driving – than the one you are facing. But it is a sharp-edged process, not a general debate about whether you are a good or bad person.

Take that stock situation that has become part of the furniture of modern Britain. Someone makes an off-the-cuff remark to which other people take offence. There are accusations of racism, sexism, homophobia, whatever. What happens next? The person accused of racism bristles with indignation. 'But I'm *not* racist.' His accusers redouble their attack. He makes a grudging, meaningless apology for any offence caused, then the circus moves on, with everyone left irritated and exhausted.

The point people miss, again and again, is that two quite distinct charges have been levelled: a serious one, racism; and a much less serious one, thoughtlessness, saying something without considering its impact. Separate those two charges, plead not guilty to the first, guilty to the second, and there is the opportunity to make a gracious, magnanimous apology. 'I'm sorry. I'm not a racist, but I should have realised my comments might offend black people and have kept my silly mouth shut. I chose my words badly.'

Nine times out of ten the apologiser will escape the main charge and win new friends with his frankness; but it is extraordinary how many people miss that opportunity, wallowing in self-righteousness instead of reaching out, in a spirit of reconciliation, to the people they have offended.

A perfect apology must start with a simple admission – that you are not perfect.

5

a question of timing

If the wording of apology requires skill, tact and imagination, the timing of an apology can be just as critical. Many a person has said sorry but gone to their grave thinking, 'If only I had said sorry *sooner*.'

Think of all those family feuds where it takes Uncle George twenty years to say sorry for calling Aunt Helen a silly cow at Uncle Henry's wedding. It suddenly dawns on the old reprobate, lying on his death bed, that although Aunt Helen *was* a silly cow, and always would be, there were probably more tactful ways of putting it; so he makes a last-gasp bid for forgiveness, like a man dashing for a train. And Aunt Helen is not such a silly cow as to spurn his apology. The need for reconciliation trumps the need for frankness.

Time heals most wounds but, if you apologise promptly, it will do its work so much quicker – whereas even a short delay can be fatal.

Even people who are fair-minded and self-critical, and do not take too long to identify situations where an apology is required, often dawdle to disastrous effect before issuing their *mea culpa*. The clock is ticking, but they do not hear it.

Glenn Hoddle, still only fifty-three and younger than Fabio Capello, might still be England football manager if he had been quicker on his feet in 1999. Hoddle had given an interview in *The Times*, published on 30 January, making comments to the effect that disabled people were being punished for sins committed in a former life. There was a predictable storm of protest and Hoddle was eventually sacked three days later, on 2 February. On the same day he issued an apology for the 'serious error of judgement' he had made in giving the interview.

I am not a fan of 'error of judgement' apologies, which always smack of euphemism and have usually been drafted by a hack lawyer. But it was Hoddle's timing that let him down on this occasion. When *The Times* interview first appeared, he tried to bluster, saying that his remarks had been 'misconstrued, misunderstood and misinterpreted'. Not good enough, Glenn. Blatant windbaggery. It was like a footballer wasting time at a throw-in. Hoddle – and, for that matter, his advisers at the FA – should have realised that a categorical apology needed to be got out as soon as possible, not seventy-two hours later. It might have defused the situation. Moral: *If you need to grovel, don't hang about.*

The England manager was guilty of a textbook error, of which history is littered with precedents. He thought he could take the public temperature and, if he needed to apologise, do so in his own good time. He did not see the danger of trying to defend an untenable position. He forgot what he should have known from long experience: that the public temperature is volatile, and goes up far quicker than it goes down.

My favourite example of an apology which came too late – making Hoddle dithering for three days look a model of decisiveness – is the 1992 apology to Galileo by Pope John Paul II on behalf of the Roman Catholic Church. The apology took a jaw-dropping 359 years to appear – comically slow going for a body that preaches the importance of contrition. Yes, that is right, 359. Even the people saying sorry for the slave trade did the decent thing after 200 years.

Galileo was tried by the Inquisition in 1633, accused of heresy for claiming that the earth moved around the sun. He was found guilty and placed under house arrest. But even after the astronomer had been proved right, his posthumous pardon took a long, long time. All right, thought the Catholic hierarchy, the Church had made a cock-up, but perhaps if one took all the relevant factors into account . . . As late as 1990, Cardinal Ratzinger, now Pope Benedict XVI, made a speech at a Rome university that appeared to endorse the view that Galileo's trial had been fairly conducted, and that it would therefore be wrong to judge his prosecutors with the wisdom of hindsight.

Some people would probably say that apologising to the dead is an exercise in futility anyway. One can imagine nineteenth-century cardinals strolling through the Vatican gardens, locked in learned theological discussion on the point. 'Galileo was right, Cardinal Tutti. The earth *does* go around the sun. Time for a *mea culpa*?' 'And have to issue *mea culpas* for all our other mistakes, Cardinal Frutti? It would be the thin end of the wedge. Let's leave it another hundred years.'

If individuals are reluctant to say sorry, the same is even more true of institutions, which stand stubbornly on their dignity, too self-important to see that a little humility would enhance that dignity ten-fold.

If you are in the wrong and everyone knows you are in the wrong – and this is true whether you are the Catholic Church bullying an astronomer or an athlete caught taking drugs – there is nothing to be said for denying the fact, and everything to be said for admitting it.

Your silence will be construed as indifference or, worse, self-right-eousness. You need to get your apology out there, even if it is not a particularly polished one. And if you think you can get away with a grudging half-apology, think again. Apologies don't work like that. There is a choreography to saying sorry that needs to be followed down to the last step. The process of forgiveness cannot begin until the words of contrition have been delivered and independently verified.

Ordinary Americans still wince at the Monica Lewinsky affair: not so much at the episode itself, as at the way it was protracted for so long that it became a national embarrassment. Even when President Clinton finally came clean about his relationship with Lewinsky, after months of denials, his first apology was so inadequate that it needed to be beefed up with subsequent supplementary apologies, dragging out the whole squalid saga even longer. Saying sorry should be a crisp, no-nonsense process, like brushing your teeth. This was a three-reel comedy.

Apology Number 1 was issued on 17 August 1998, after the president had testified to the Grand Jury:

> 'I did have a relationship with Miss Lewinsky that was not appropriate. In fact, it was wrong. It constituted a critical lapse in judgement and a personal failure on my part for which I am solely and completely responsible . . . I misled many people, including even my wife. I deeply regret that.'

Nobody was buying *that*. Critical lapse of judgement, indeed! The phrase was comically out of kilter with the stained dresses and other minutiae of the Lewinsky affair.

Apology Number 2, issued on 4 September, was only marginally better:

> 'I made a big mistake. It is indefensible and I am sorry.'

Still no good, not by a long chalk. If the president thought what he had done in the Oval Office could be passed off as a mistake, that was his biggest mistake yet. Spilling *coffee* on Monica Lewinsky's dress, now, that would have been a mistake. By belittling his offence the president was implicitly defending something he had said was indefensible.

It was only with Apology Number 3, issued a week later on 11 September, that Clinton finally hit his straps:

> 'I agree with those who have said that, in my first statement after I testified, I was not contrite enough. I don't think there is a fancy way to say that I have sinned. It is important to me that everybody who has been hurt know that the sorrow I feel is genuine: first and most important, my family; also my friends, my staff, the Cabinet, Monica Lewinsky and her family; and the American people. I have asked all for their forgiveness.'

A bit more of the same, some judicious references to God, which played well in the Bible Belt, and the president was off the hook, his misdemeanours forgiven, if not forgotten. The real masterstroke in the apology was the word 'sinned'. It is simply not a word you expect to hear from politicians. It has the power of simplicity.

Whether or not the president was truly contrite is between him and his Maker, but he *sounded* contrite. Clinton never quite regained the authority he had enjoyed in his first presidency, but he had re-established his reputation as a good communicator, a politician who, like Ronald Reagan, could connect with voters because he spoke their language. After months of acting like the Arkansas lawyer he was – minding his back, denying liability, only admitting what could be proved against him – he remembered that he was a human being.

On this side of the Atlantic, the slowest politician out of the traps when it comes to apologising – against stiff competition – has to be ex-London Mayor Ken Livingstone, who has such a deep-seated phobia of the s-word that there should be a medical condition named after him.

In February 2005, Livingstone likened an *Evening Standard* reporter to 'a concentration-camp guard', insulting not just the reporter, but millions of others. Somewhere deep inside that thick skull, a voice must have been whispering: 'Steady on, Ken. That was a bit over the top.' But did Livingstone listen to that voice? No way. It was not until the furore had rumbled on for nearly two years that he climbed down, apologising for his comment in a speech at the London Jewish Forum. By that time, of course, it was too late. His political support had haemorrhaged, not least because of this unedifying incident.

The subsequent mayoral election in 2008 threw up a contest that had students of political apologies rubbing their hands in anticipation. In the red corner, Ken Livingstone, the mule who would never apologise; in the blue corner, Boris Johnson, the ass who could not apologise enough. Fittingly, it was the ass – asses in power are far less dangerous than mules in power – who won.

Boris Johnson has had so much practice at apologising that he should be rather good at it by now. In fact, he makes the same schoolboy errors again and again, meaning well, but rarely getting his apologies spot-on. But the fact that he is patently a good sport, able to laugh at himself, plays well with voters.

Who can forget his pilgrimage of contrition to Liverpool in 2004, after he had outraged Liverpudlians with an article published in the *Spectator*, and was required to apologise to the city in person by Michael Howard, the Tory party leader at the time? It was the *locus classicus* of the public apology as pantomime. How the **** does one apologise to a city in person? Johnson ended up checking into a hotel as Mr Birkenshaw, which gave the press a field day. But to my mind, it was still preferable to the apology delayed for months, if not years.

None of this is rocket science. The longer you delay an apology – and this is true whether you are London mayor, the American president, or someone who has had a row with a work colleague – the harder it is to make the apology sound convincing. Your prevarication will inevitably create the suspicion that you are trying to get away with *not* apologising. The other person is likely to conclude that you do not think you have done anything wrong or, worse, are indifferent to the fact that you have hurt their feelings. Once such perceptions have taken root, they can be very, very hard to shift.

Far more will be expected of an apology that has taken weeks to deliver than of one that is delivered promptly. The recipient will pore over it, suspicious of its motives, alert to any deficiencies in the wording. So why hang about? If you know you are going to have to say sorry at some point, it is best to apologise sooner rather than later. It is the needs of the *other* person, the one to whom you are apologising, that should be paramount. If you think, 'Well, I'm seeing them next Thursday, I can eat humble pie then,' you are following your own timetable, not theirs, and they will not thank you for it. Far better to show them how much you value their friendship with the promptness of your apology.

People issuing written apologies make the same elementary mistake again and again. They delude themselves that if they spend days working on their apology they will be able to produce a better-worded apology. Apologies don't work like that. Language doesn't work like that. A first draft of an apology is rarely perfect, so the first re-write is usually an improvement; but after four or five re-writes, there is a law of diminishing returns, as the writer succumbs to over-elaboration.

I hate to think how many re-writes were needed before Tiger Woods issued his infamous apology on 1 December 2009. The golfer had been caught cheating on his wife, had a domestic row, then smashed his car driving away from his Florida home at two in the morning. So he had plenty of explaining to do. But the five days Woods allowed himself to compose his apology – with the sporting world holding its breath – practically guaranteed that it would be a turkey. And it was. The very first sentence was off-key:

'I have let my family down and regret those transgressions with all
of my heart.'

Transgressions? What a very Victorian way of putting it. And which
transgressions was Woods talking about? The apology begged more
questions than it answered. Elsewhere in the statement there were
coy references to 'personal sins', grudging admissions that he was 'not
perfect' (as if anyone had thought he was), angry pleas for privacy,
then a 'profound apology' to everyone who had supported him over
the years – though still no explanation of what he was apologising
for. It was like watching a twenty-four-handicap golfer hack from one
side of the fairway to the other.

One could sense the laboriousness of the whole process, with
the golfer sitting around a table with lawyers and press officers and
sports psychologists, trying out different forms of words, hoping to
come up with the right one. Woods should have issued a simpler
apology sooner.

His later efforts to repair the damage – including a public apology
that became one of the media events of 2010 – only emphasised the
danger of delay. Nearly three months passed while the golfer went
into hiding, sought treatment for sex addiction and tried to mend
fences with his wife. Then, on 19 February 2010, having had time to
script, stage-manage and choreograph a suitable public apology, he
faced the public again.

What a circus! His scripted fourteen-minute speech was not
actually too bad; there were three uses of the s-word and enough
self-flagellation to satisfy a medieval monk. It was a carefully crafted
piece of work – as could only be expected after that length of time.
But the delivery was quite awful: so robotic that the robot became
the story, not the words the robot was using. Some commentators
compared Woods to a speaking clock, but that is being unfair to

speaking clocks. There have actually been some quite expressive speaking clocks over the years, particularly in the days when the job went to a nice gal from the Home Counties.

Woods and his advisers had missed the bleeding obvious. If someone has a ten-foot putt to win the Masters, what is the cruellest thing you can do to them? Make them wait. And wait. And wait. The longer they have to think about the putt, the more likely they are to miss it, as the pressure builds up in their brain. Apologising is no different. The reason Woods was frozen with misery on his big day was simple: his big day came too late.

Of course, there is no point in lurching from one extreme to another. If delaying an apology can be fatal, the same is true, to a lesser extent, of apologising too quickly. There are some contexts where an instant 'Sorry!' is advisable, even obligatory, e.g., if you have just knocked over a wine glass and spilled Chateau Lafitte '87 on your hostess's carpet; but in more complex situations, apologising too precipitately can make things worse rather than better.

If the offence is serious enough, there needs to be a time lag between the commission of the offence and the admission of wrongdoing: a period of sober reflection on the hurt you have caused. If you simply apologise the moment you realise you have upset someone – and, by implication, expect instant forgiveness – you are on shaky ground. A quick-fire apology will come across as glib, premature, ill-considered – like a proposal of marriage made to someone you have only known for a week. It debases the currency.

I have an old friend who is always late for our meetings. I stopped trying to work out why twenty years ago – let us just say that he has time-management issues – but his zeal for apologising is undimmed. In fact, the apologies arrive before he does. 'Incredibly sorry' will come the text message from the motorway that is forever jinxed by five-mile tailbacks, or from the train that has been stuck in fog at

Reading since 1981. Pre-texting, he used to come puffing down my street, calling out 'Sorry!' in a theatrical croak, like a homing pigeon with laryngitis. I love him to bits, but the instant s-words, pre-empting my complaints, add insult to injury.

The latest fad, symptomatic of an impatient age, is apologising on Twitter. Some people rush out their apologies so quickly that the readers of their tweets have no idea why they are apologising. The intention behind the apologies may be good, but their execution usually leaves a lot to be desired. Nine times out ten, they only sow confusion.

Take the sad case of Hull City footballer Jozy Altidore, a young American international, just out of his teens. In October 2009, Altidore reported so late for a match against Portsmouth that his manager, Phil Brown, had no choice but to leave him out of the side. The American sent out an instant tweet: 'Apologise to the all of you. I showed up late. Made a big mistake. I'm very very sorry.' As apologies go, it is not too bad, far better than one of those serpentine lawyer's apologies (note the postmodern artfulness with which the author creates a sense of raw emotion through illiterate syntax), but Twitter was a poor choice of medium, if only because tweets, which are limited in length, are so cursory. Why was the footballer late? That is the main question Hull City fans wanted answered. No explanation is given. Altidore's manager was certainly not amused by the tweet. The player was punished twice: once for being late and once for washing the club's dirty linen in public.

Philosopher Alain de Botton uses language so much more elegantly than Altidore that they could be members of different species, but when it comes to apologising, their instincts are identical. *Just say you're sorry. Get it off your chest.* In April 2009, the normally cerebral writer astonished the literary world with an intemperate attack on an American critic who had been rude about one of his books. As the storm raged above his head, de Botton felt so wretched that he went on Twitter, not once, but more than once. One tweet quoted Montaigne, which must have been a Twitter first: 'To learn we have said a stupid thing is nothing. We must learn a more ample, important lesson: we are but blockheads.' Another was more personal: 'I was so wrong, so un-self-controlled. Now I am sorry and ashamed of myself.'

The urge to atone was evident, and laudable, but the tweets, by their very peremptoriness, could not do justice to the atonement. If anything, they undermined de Botton's well-earned reputation as a high priest of rational discourse.

Still, like Altidore, he had erred on the right side. It would have been so easy for him to keep his counsel, wait a week, then make a mature, considered apology in the *Observer*, full of all the right sentiments, with not a word out of place. That's what 90 per cent of writers would have done in the same situation. But I'm with de Botton, not the 90 per cent. Sometimes, just from the reaction of other people, you know immediately that you have done something wrong. So why not act on that knowledge? A week is a long time in the contrition business.

Context is all. When French footballer Thierry Henry cheated Ireland out of a place in the 2010 World Cup finals by deliberately handling the ball in a play-off in Paris, his apology appeared on Twitter within hours. 'I'm not the referee . . . but if I hurt someone, I am sorry.' Too late. The time for Henry to apologise was within seconds of handling the ball. That way the goal could have been disallowed and he would not have profited from his cheating. Delaying the apology until it was of no practical consequence made him a hypocrite as well as a cheat.

Football fans are no fools: they know crocodile tears when they see them. As for the wording of the apology, the less said the better. 'If I hurt someone . . .' *If*? With five million Irishmen spitting blood? A sporting reputation lay in ruins – not because of the handball itself, but because of the tardiness of the apology.

Apologising promptly is particularly important when the original offence was of the rush-of-blood-to-the-head variety. If you have lost your temper with someone and snapped some' outrageous insult at them, the time to say sorry is as soon as your temper has cooled, within minutes. To dawdle for days gives the impression that you are too bone-headed to see that you have been out of order.

Serena Williams shocked the tennis world in the final of the 2009 US Open, when she screamed an x-rated volley of abuse at a lineswoman who had foot-faulted her on match point. But it was thirty-six hours before this feeble backhand of an apology limped over the net: 'I want to sincerely apologise for my inappropriate outburst. I'm a woman of great pride, faith and integrity, and I admit when I'm wrong.' Yuk. The split infinitive in the first sentence could be forgiven, at a pinch; but not the dilatoriness, or the arrogance behind it.

Given the venom with which the player had laid into the lineswoman, the time to apologise was immediately after the incident – no ifs, no buts. Instead, Williams tried to brazen it out at her post-match press conference, saying that she had no regrets – that cheesy old Piaf line which always sounds great for a couple of seconds before revealing its absurdity. Edith Piaf has a lot to answer for; you could fill the Albert Hall with people who have stolen her line, when they should have known better.

For a sportswoman who had been admired, if not loved, Williams trashed her good name in breathtaking fashion. You can almost measure the extent of her stupidity in mathematical terms, the way you can measure the speed of her serve. Between her outburst at the lineswoman and her eventual apology, nearly thirty-six hours, or around 2,000 minutes, elapsed. In every single one of those minutes there would have been thousands of fans – say, two thousand, for the sake of argument – whose opinion of Serena Williams fell as they digested this unsavoury episode, watching television replays or reading about it on the internet. That adds up to four million fans, which, given the worldwide tennis audience, is probably an underestimate.

Now take away the people who thought better of Serena Williams because of the episode. Six? Seven? Her coach, her father, her sister, a few half-wits in California? That still leaves three million, nine hundred and ninety-nine thousand, nine hundred and ninety-something people whose goodwill was squandered – all because of a failure to issue a prompt, unequivocal apology.

One should beware of generalisations, but in most situations where an apology is called for, the best time to issue the apology is not when it suits you, but when it will be most appreciated by the recipient. That could be a matter of seconds after the original offence – if you have sworn at a stranger in the street, say – or many years after the original offence – for instance, if you are a mother who has given up a baby for adoption and been reunited with it as an adult. But in either event, the timing matters almost as much as the wording.

Get it wrong, and it doesn't matter if your apology reads like the Gettysburg Address. People won't totally trust it.

Get it right, and any blemishes in the apology will be overlooked, as the recipient hugs it gratefully to their bosom.

6

the seven deadly sins of apologising

There are so many ways to botch an apology that in referring to seven deadly sins, errors to be avoided at all costs, I am probably guilty of under-accounting. But these are, if you like, the classic misuses of the s-word: schoolboy howlers that you encounter again and again, often in combination with each other – particularly if the apologiser is a lawyer, a politician or an employee of British Gas.

1. The Apology That Doubles as an Excuse

We have all heard them: those apologies that begin well, with a pretty show of contrition, then run into the sands as the apologiser stops saying sorry, which is the object of the exercise, and starts making excuses, which are neither here nor there. It is a human enough thing to do. If a man has cheated on his wife when he was not just drunk, but tired, under pressure at work, and stranded in Wolverhampton on a wet Wednesday, he wants each separate mitigating factor to be taken into account. But there is a time and a place for the pleas in mitigation, and it is not during the sackcloth-and-ashes phase of the apology.

Explanations, within reason, are fine. In fact, some apologies ('I'm sorry I'm late') are incomplete without some kind of explanation.

But as you soon as you start elaborating on an explanation you are on a slippery slope, hurtling downhill towards a pathetic, risible excuse.

Not many people slide as far down the slope as actor Russell Crowe, who, after throwing a telephone at a desk clerk in a New York hotel in 2005, blamed 'jet lag, loneliness and adrenalin', a triple-decker excuse of awesome proportions. But it is extraordinary how often people ruin what might otherwise be an acceptable apology by overdoing the excuses.

Here is a classic case of an apology and an excuse becoming fatally intertwined. In September 2009, Baroness Scotland, Attorney General at the time, was in hot water after inadvertently employing an illegal immigrant as her housekeeper. She should have kept a photocopy of the housekeeper's passport details, but omitted to do so. Embarrassingly, she had breached regulations passed by her own government, and for this was fined £5,000.

When challenged about the case on *Sky News*, the Baroness had this to say:

'I made an administrative, technical error for which I am bitterly, bitterly sorry. I will never fail to take a photocopy again. It was a technical breach and I have paid the penalty.'

It doesn't quite work, does it? The repeated 'bitterly' is terrific, it is like a line from Greek tragedy; it should be set to music, with a video montage of the Baroness wailing and beating her breast. But the repeated 'technical' undoes all the good work. A strong show of remorse is diluted, contradicted, by an insipid excuse.

Or how about this shocker of an apology from Chris Tarrant? In 2006, the TV presenter was revealed to have had a long-running relationship with a schoolteacher, which put paid to his marriage.

He wanted to make an emotional public apology to his wife Ingrid and, if you take out the words I have italicised, made a reasonable fist of it:

> 'I am deeply sorry for the hurt I have caused to my loyal wife and wonderful children, all of whom I adore. I have only myself to blame for the breakdown of my marriage. *While the liaison which has led to all of this was not significant in my life*, I will always regret the hurt and pain which I have caused to those whom I love.'

Not significant? What planet is the man living on? If the liaison ended his marriage, it was very significant, by definition. With his unhappy choice of word, Tarrant has managed to insult his wife *and* the other woman: a double-whammy so clumsy it makes you wince just reading it. The excuse has a desperate quality, as if the apologiser cannot bear the thought of having no excuse for his behaviour, so he clutches at the only excuse he can think of, however threadbare, then crowbars it into the apology at the last minute.

Apologising and excuse-making are two sides of the same coin. The best are guilty of it. I am sorry to disabuse empty-headed women whose romantic ideal of manhood is Mr Darcy in *Pride and Prejudice*, but for connoisseurs of rickety excuses, Mr D comes up with an absolute pearler, Tarrant-esque in its inadequacy:

> 'As a child I was taught what was right, but I was not taught to correct my temper. I was given good principles, but left to follow them in pride and conceit. Unfortunately an only son, I was spoilt by my parents who, though good themselves, allowed, encouraged, almost taught me to be selfish and overbearing.'

Ah, so it was his *parents* who made him so insufferable – and an only child, too, poor lamb. If a defendant tried that one in the Ealing magistrates' court, he would get very short shrift from the bench. Elizabeth should have left Darcy on the discard pile, where he belonged.

Some excuses are so lame that they make a complete nonsense of the apology. Here is actress Sienna Miller grovelling after being rude to bar staff in Pittsburgh, Pennsylvania, in 2006:

> 'I'm very sorry about being rude, but I was working so hard on the movie, *The Mysteries of Pittsburgh*. I was tired and it came out wrong. I feel terrible about it.'

The real gem in this is the comically imprecise phrase, 'It came out wrong', worthy of a *Carry On* film. Miller should, by rights, have been honing up her skills as an apologiser. While filming the same movie she had already had to issue one apology, for referring to Pittsburgh as 'Sh*tsburgh' in a magazine interview.

Some excuses are so laughable that you find yourself warming to the people who dream them up. In June 2009, Swaziland MP Timothy Myeni – a pastor as well as a politician – was forced to apologise after suggesting that AIDS sufferers should be branded on the buttocks to alert their partners to their condition. Myeni duly coughed up the s-word, but could not resist this cunning rider:

> 'Maybe it was a trap from the Devil to destroy my name.'

Ridiculous, yes, but full marks for ingenuity.

If there is anything worse than making feeble excuses, it is making feeble excuses after promising that you are not going to make feeble excuses. Spot the glaring non sequitur in this torrent of waffle from

Christian Bale in February 2009, after footage had been released of the actor having a hissy fit on set during the filming of *Terminator Salvation*:

> 'I was out of order beyond belief. I was way out of order. I acted like a punk. I regret that . . . I make no excuses for it, it is inexcusable, and I hope that is absolutely clear. One thing that has really disturbed me throughout this is I'm not familiar or comfortable with this notion of being a movie star. I'm an actor and I don't quite know how to handle it.'

The speed with which the excuse follows the promises not to make excuses is reminiscent of the famous occasion on which Tony Blair said it was no time for sound bites but he felt the hand of history on his shoulder. Delicious.

2. The Conditional Apology

Saying sorry is, or should be, a pure act, like making a declaration of love. If you have to qualify it, or make it conditional, you are copping out. That is why any apology, spoken or written, which contains the word 'if' should be distrusted on principle. There is the odd exception to the rule, but by and large, as soon as you start qualifying your apology, you are weakening its impact.

Lurking inside contrite-sounding sentences like 'I am sorry if I have upset you' is the forlorn hope that the whole thing has been some ghastly misunderstanding and you will be let off the hook without having to buy a bunch of flowers as a peace offering.

Apologies of the 'I'm sorry if have upset you' variety, and they are two a penny, tend to be not just weakly phrased, and therefore ineffective, but also exercises in blame-shifting. The tone is conciliatory, but the subtext is grudging, even hostile. *I suppose, if you are so pathetic as to take offence, I had better backtrack.*

Here is Cherie Blair in December 2002, making a tearful public apology during the furore caused by her links with convicted Australian conman Peter Foster, who had helped her buy some flats in Bristol:

> 'I'm sorry if I have embarrassed anyone, but the people who know me well know that I would never want to harm anyone, least of all Tony, or the children, or the Labour government, or misuse my position in any way at all.'

This is such a soggy mess of an apology, positively marinating in self-pity, that if one did not know the woman, or know lawyers, it would be hard to credit that the words had been drafted by a highly paid QC. The 'if' cripples the whole sentence, even before it gets on to the pleas in mitigation. She *had* embarrassed her husband, full stop.

There was another celebrated 'if' which should have got the red-pencil treatment in President Nixon's televised speech to the nation on the night he resigned the Presidency in August 1974:

> 'I regret deeply any injuries that may have been done in the course of events that have led to this decision. I would say only that, if some of my judgments were wrong, and they were wrong, they were made in what I believed at the time to be in the best interest of the nation.'

Again, as with Cherie Blair, the 'if' is only part of a much broader failure to call a spade a spade. What an awkward, crablike communicator Nixon was. And another lawyer, too! Well, there's a coincidence.

Prince Charles is not a lawyer, of course, but in his speech to the Royal Institute of British Architects in May 2009, in a clumsy effort to atone for his infamous 'carbuncle' remark a quarter of a century earlier, he slipped in an 'if' like a seasoned QC:

> 'I am sorry if somehow I left the faintest impression that I wished to kick-start some kind of style war between classicists and modernists, or that I somehow wanted to drag the world back to the eighteenth century.'

This is a pretty feeble effort all round, even without the 'if'. It is just so weakly worded, with all those limp-wristed qualifiers: 'somehow', 'some kind of', 'somehow' again. The Prince should have stuck to his guns and called a carbuncle a carbuncle.

Some apologisers insert an 'if' in their apologies deliberately, giving ground, but in such a resentful, truculent way that they reveal their contempt for the person demanding the apology. You can almost hear the sneer in this statement issued by England cricket captain Michael Atherton in 1999, after he had caused an uproar by calling a Pakistani journalist a 'buffoon' during a press conference:

> 'I'm sorry if I caused offence to a local journalist.'

If he had caused offence? Atherton knew damn well he had caused offence. What is the point of calling someone a buffoon if not to offend them? The England captain did the decent thing, up to a point, but his apology did little to defuse the diplomatic incident he had provoked.

In some hands, a sly conditional clause in an apology can be playful, even elegant. I like this ingenious 2007 apology from David Van

Day, the former pop singer, who, while standing as a Conservative candidate in Brighton, upset a homosexual man in the audience with an off-colour joke about a gay men's choir:

'If that chap is sincerely offended, then I sincerely apologise to him.'

Neat, very neat, like a crisp cross-court volley at tennis. It reminds me of an equally elegant remark attributed to D.H. Lawrence: 'If I've done anything I'm sorry for, I'm willing to be forgiven.' In the right context, there is nothing wrong with a leavening of humour: it makes the apology harder to reject.

No such elegance can be discerned in this gangly pantomime horse of an apology from former Olympics Minister Tessa Jowell as she tried to appease Labour Party activists at the height of the parliamentary expenses scandal:

'If you feel that we, the government, fall short of what you expect, then I say sorry for that.'

Come again, Tessa? Everything about the sentence is off-key. From the moment the minister starts the sentence with an 'if', she is heading down a cul-de-sac of her own making. By the time she gets to the s-word, there is nothing to say sorry for, because she has sneakily shifted responsibility from the government to voters and their *expectations* of the government.

Her cabinet colleague Andy Burnham made an equally poor fist of his letter of apology to Shami Chakrabarti in June 2008, after he had accused the Liberty director of having 'late-night, hand-wringing, heart-melting' phone conversations with a Tory MP:

'The very last thing I set out to do was to cause any personal offence to you, your family or any other party. If this is what has happened by the misinterpretation of my remarks, then I regret that.'

What a joke. It is like a car running out of petrol. After the bombastic opening ('The very last thing . . .'), the apology just fizzles out, with a string of weasel words and caveats. As soon as apologisers start protesting that their words have been misinterpreted, their contrition invariably has a hollow ring. Burnham should have kept it simple, admitted he had chosen his words badly, and left it at that.

3. Crocodile Tears

Call me a cynic, but I am always sceptical about apologies delivered on a flood tide of emotion. If you are truly contrite, it is the hurt you have caused the other person, and *their* emotions – not your own distress, genuine though it might be – that should have priority. To turn your apology into a self-serving pantomime of grief is a form of discourtesy. You need to demonstrate remorse – that goes without saying – but it must not be remorse of the theatrical, exaggerated kind. A little sobriety is required.

When Sir Fred Goodwin, the disgraced former boss of RBS, was hauled before the Treasury Committee with his fellow bankers in February 2009, the stage should have been set for the mother and father of apologies. It was common knowledge that Sir Fred had been rehearsing his lines with advisers beforehand, going through possible forms of words. So it should have been, at worst, a well-crafted apology: a professional *mea culpa* rather than an amateurish grovel. Instead, ludicrously, we got this:

'I could not be more sorry about what has happened.'

The apology has a grandiloquent ring, but the grandiloquence is 99 per cent vanity. *Look at me! I am the sorriest banker in the world! Nobody could be sorrier than Fred Goodwin!*

When push came to shove, and attention shifted to Sir Fred's obscenely large pension, the tenacity with which he tried to defend his pension rights showed the banker in his true colours. He simply could not see that an apology needs to be followed by a commensurate act of reparation. It is not just words in a vacuum.

Judging whether an apologiser is truly contrite, or just putting on a performance, is an inexact science, but there are a number of telltale signs. Watch out in particular for superfluous adverbs. 'I'm really sorry' is fine. 'I'm really really sorry' is flannel. The apologiser is just sexing up the apology to disguise its other shortcomings.

Adverb-counters will have enjoyed this *mea culpa* from another banker, John Varley, the Barclays Chief Executive. As the credit crunch started to bite, Varley was one of the first top British bankers to appreciate that a show of contrition was expected from the City. But his own efforts were long on bluster, short on substance:

'Am I sorry for what has happened? Unambiguously and unequivocally, yes.'

The 'unambiguously' he might have got away with, but as soon as he added the 'unequivocally', one smelled a rat. The orotund adverbs cunningly masked the fact that, apology or no apology, Varley had no intention of admitting to any specific financial wrongdoing by Barclays. In fact, there was a gaping ambiguity at the heart of the apology. For what, if anything, was Varley apologising?

The more fulsome the crocodile tears, as a rule, the flakier the apology. Listen to this incontinent rant on Facebook from jobbing celebrity Kerry Katona, after the former member of Atomic Kitten had been exposed in the *News of the World*, apparently snorting cocaine:

> 'I just want to say how sorry, ashamed and embarrassed I am over my recent actions in the press. I have let a lot of people down, my (so-called) fans (what's left of them), my work colleagues and more so my family.'

This one breaks so many of the rules of apologising that it would be tedious to enumerate them. For the connoisseur, the real gem is the phrase, 'over my recent actions in the press', which is so woolly it should be knitted into a jumper. In a sense, the raw emotion of the wording is preferable to the dry circumlocutions of lawyers. But is Katona really sorry? It is impossible to tell through the mist of tears.

The acid test of an apology is its humility, or lack of it. If a scintilla of vanity creeps into an apology, it is worthless.

In October 2009, when former Home Secretary Jacqui Smith was forced to apologise to the House of Commons after being censured for wrongly claiming expenses on her second home, her choice of words was comically self-regarding:

> 'I want to apologise to my constituents. They are my main priority, and for too long this investigation has been allowed to overshadow the work I do for them.'

The *work she did for them*, note, not the money they contributed as tax-payers to her expenses, which was the real nub of the issue.

At least Jacqui Smith kept her apology reasonably brief. In the States, interminable self-serving apologies, with the celebrity-penitent hogging the limelight for as long as possible, have become one of the curses of the age. Here is an absolute Niagara of crocodile tears from disgraced American athlete Marion Jones in October 2007, after the one-time Olympic gold-medallist had been exposed as a drug cheat:

> 'Good afternoon, everyone. I am Marion Jones-Thompson, and I am here today because I have something very important to tell you, my fans, my friends and my family.
>
> Over the many years of my life, as an athlete in track and field, you have been fiercely loyal and supportive towards me. Even more loyal and supportive than words can declare has been my family, and especially my dear mother, who stands by my side today.
>
> And so it with a great amount of shame that I stand before you and tell you that I have betrayed your trust. I want you all to know that today I plead guilty to two counts of making false statements to federal agents . . .
>
> To you, my fans, including my young supporters, the United States Track and Field Association, my closest friends, my attorneys, and the most classy family a person could ever hope for, namely, my mother, my husband, my children, my brother and his family, my uncle, and the rest of my extended family . . .'

As relative follows relative, and you start thinking, 'Is that the lot? Hasn't she left out some second cousins somewhere?', a show of contrition that began quite well plummets into farce.

4. Deflecting the Blame

One of the classic tactics of the apologiser is to shift the focus of attention away from themselves. Ever since Adam grassed on Eve in the Garden of Eden ('The woman gave to me and I did eat'), people caught with their trousers down, their foot in their mouth or their hands in the till have hunted around for scapegoats.

Such diversionary tactics can take many different forms, and when someone has long experience of apologising, like gaffe-prone London Mayor Boris Johnson, they develop an impressive range of blame-shifting ploys.

At one end of the scale is the simple passing of the buck. *It was not my fault. It was their fault.* Here is the mayor in June 2009, saying sorry to London commuters whose journeys had been delayed by a Tube strike:

> 'I apologise for the disruption, but I must say I lay the blame squarely at the door of the extremely ill-advised leadership of the RMT.'

Not elegant, perhaps, but certainly lucid.

Here, in quite different vein, is Johnson in September 2006, using heavy sarcasm to backtrack after controversial off-the-cuff remarks imputing cannibalism to the people of Papua New Guinea:

> 'I meant no insult to the people of Papua New Guinea, who I'm sure lead lives of blameless bourgeois domesticity in common with the rest of us.'

His first joke had backfired, so he tried a second joke to repair the damage. *Not* recommended. Any Papua New Guineans offended by the first joke would hardly have been appeased by the second.

If it is any consolation to the London mayor, he is in good company. Listen to this classic piece of blame shifting by Pope Benedict XVI, whom I took to task earlier in the book. In September 2007, in a speech at Regensburg University in Germany, His Holiness sparked a storm of protest in the Muslim world by – pretty naively, it must be said – quoting from a medieval text hostile to Islam. His speech was misreported, the nuances of his argument were lost in translation, and all hell broke loose, from Morocco to Indonesia, until the Pope had to make a public apology:

> 'I am deeply sorry for the reactions in some countries to a few passages of my address at the University of Regensburg, which were considered offensive to the sensibility of Muslims.'

What sort of an apology is that? His Holiness was speaking in Italian, so perhaps something has got lost in translation. But whether he was speaking in English, Italian or Swahili, the whole thinking behind the apology was awry. It is a fudge, a cop-out, a smoke-and-mirrors job, simulating remorse but not demonstrating remorse. The Pope might, at very least, have conceded that his speech had been ineptly drafted, inviting misinterpretation. Saying sorry for the reactions of *other people* to the speech was, well, the sort of thing Members of Parliament do.

During the storm over MPs' expenses in 2009, so many of the worst offenders tried to deflect the blame on to someone else – usually the House of Commons Fees Office, although the nasty, intrusive media were also invoked – that it was like watching a game of pass-the-parcel. Tory MPs Andrew MacKay and his wife Julie Kirkbride were found to have used the expenses system to claim for two separate second homes, which seemed to call for a gushing apology from someone. Instead, MacKay told his constituency association:

> 'I am sorry we have all become embroiled in this expenses row, particularly as I was following advice.'

This was not just a particularly sly and unrepentant use of the s-word, but a blatant attempt to point the finger of blame at the parliamentary officials who had approved his claims – claims he should never have had the gall to make in the first place. Few tears were shed when MacKay was forced to stand down as an MP.

At a human level, it is easy to see why some apologisers feel like cornered animals, and act accordingly, lashing out at their attackers at the same time as they are saying sorry. But it is not smart to send two totally contradictory messages; any reputation you have for sincerity will lie in shreds.

In April 2007, after Richard Gere had caused a furore in India by ostentatiously kissing Bollywood star Shilpa Shetty at an event promoting AIDS awareness, the actor only made things worse with the coiled-up belligerence of his apology:

'I apologise to the people of India and especially actress Shilpa Shetty for my recent behaviour. I have spent a great amount of time in India over the years, so I can neither defend nor explain my lack of understanding of your culture, as repressed and antiquated as it is. I also understand that the enormous amounts of time and money I have devoted towards saving the Indian people from poverty and death will do nothing to alleviate the great offence I have inflicted upon you. It is my humble pledge to no longer insult the integrity of the people of India through my tireless charity work, when it is clear that they would prefer the abject misery of an AIDS epidemic to the threat of further displays of affection by an ignorant foreigner.'

The sarcastic tone was not going to endear the actor to anyone. He should have identified what, if anything, he wanted to say sorry for, issued that apology, then made his wider point about Indian cultural attitudes in a different forum.

5. The Watered-down Apology

A good apology should be like a malt whisky: silky-smooth on the palate because so much love and care has gone into its preparation. Add a splash of warm tap water and you ruin it.

Listen to Michael Martin, former Speaker of the House of Commons, apologising to the nation in May 2009 for the parliamentary expenses scandal:

> 'I want to say to the men and women of the United Kingdom that we have let you down very badly indeed and, *to the extent that I've contributed to that situation*, I'm profoundly sorry.'

It is the words I have italicised which kill this apology. You can see the thinking behind them and, to an extent, sympathise with it: the Speaker wanted to express his contrition, but also make clear that, as far he was concerned, he was not the only MP at fault. But the whole parabola of the sentence, with that surreptitious qualifying clause, is wrong. It hints at a cop-out. It is as if the apologiser is saying: 'Well, I suppose I'd better grovel, but nobody's going to pin all the blame for this shambles on *me*.'

There are so many ways to water down an apology that it is impossible to list them all. One of the most common is to slip in little qualifying phrases such as 'with hindsight', or 'in retrospect', or 'on reflection'. The phrases are totally redundant: if you are apologising for something you have done, your apology is retrospective, by definition. But it is extraordinary how many apologisers throw in such meaningless, mealy-mouthed phrases, as if clutching at a fig leaf to hide their embarrassment.

When Jeremy Clarkson caused outrage during a visit to Australia in 2009 by referring to Gordon Brown as 'a one-eyed Scottish idiot', even that emotional rhinoceros realised he had overstepped the mark and would have to backtrack. But what a D-reg Ford Escort of an apology the presenter of *Top Gear* came up with:

'In the heat of the moment, I made a remark about the prime minister's personal appearance for which, on reflection, I apologise.'

It is the *faux*-philosophical 'on reflection', redolent of a Victorian vicar sipping sherry in his carpet slippers, that derails this apology. Clarkson was not remotely contrite. In fact, he later told the *Sun*: 'I haven't apologised for calling Brown an idiot.' How graceless can you get?

Watered-down apologies, with their timid interpolations, are as English as weak tea. Here is Buckingham Palace in 1999, issuing one of its regulation apologies for a gaffe by the Duke of Edinburgh. On a visit to an electronics factory, the Duke had reportedly said of a faulty installation: 'It looks as though it was put in by an Indian.' Panic stations! Man the lifeboats! You can almost hear the flap of courtiers rummaging through filing cabinets, looking for the last post-gaffe apology so that they could rehash it. But even after long years of practice the Palace was not able to get the wording right:

'The Duke of Edinburgh regrets any offence which may have been caused by remarks he is reported as making earlier today. With hindsight, he accepts that what were intended as light-hearted comments were inappropriate.'

Take away 'with hindsight', which makes the Duke sound vaguely half-witted, and the effect is so much better. The 'inappropriate' is also wide of the mark, bringing an insipid apology to a watery conclusion. The word is widely used by apologisers, particularly ones acting on legal advice, but it smacks of euphemism every time you hear it. If something is merely inappropriate it is not a hanging offence, just a small social lapse, like wearing brown shoes with black trousers, barely worth apologising for. Stronger language was called for on this occasion.

In fact, show me someone who admits to having done something 'inappropriate' and I will show you someone in denial. In 2008, actress Sharon Stone caused a storm of protest after telling an interviewer that China, which had just been struck by an earthquake, was suffering karmic reward for its treatment of Tibet. Her subsequent apology fell well short of what was required:

'Due to my inappropriate words during the interview, I feel deeply sorry and sad about hurting Chinese people.'

Change 'inappropriate' to 'insensitive' or, better still, 'crassly insensitive', and the apology holds water.

Here is an equally inept use of the word by easyJet, who should be world-champion apologisers, with all the experience they have had of leaving passengers stranded in dodgy French airports without their luggage:

'We profusely apologise to anyone who may be offended by the inappropriate fashion photo shoot at the Holocaust Memorial in Berlin featured in this month's issue of the in-flight magazine.'

You do not need to know the full background to grasp why this is such a turkey of an apology. All the information you need can be found in the choice and sequence of words ('inappropriate . . . fashion shoot . . . Holocaust Memorial'). To anyone with half an ear, 'inappropriate' just sounds wrong.

Equally objectionable is that ghastly portmanteau phrase, 'error of judgement', much favoured by makers of apologies, who seem to view it as an elegant halfway house: a climb-down of sorts, but not an out-and-out grovel.

Verbally, 'I made an error of judgement' sounds stronger than 'I made a mistake', but once you unpick the phrase it amounts to the same thing. The subtext is the same in each case: *I didn't have my brain in gear, but that doesn't mean I'm a bad or malicious person. I just screwed up.*

Depending on the circumstances, you can get away with admitting to an error of judgement, if the offence is sufficiently trivial. But it is a dangerous game to play. In October 2008, after Jonathan Ross and Russell Brand had caused outrage with their infamous phone call to Andrew Sachs, in which they made lewd sexual comments about his granddaughter, Ross tried to defuse the situation by admitting to 'a stupid error of judgement'. Not good enough, not nearly good enough – even with the 'stupid' added. Ross's error was not one of judgement, but of taste, respect, good manners and ordinary human decency. The apology should have matched the offence, not been toned down, which cast doubt on its sincerity.

So, is 'I made a mistake' better than 'I made an error of judgement'? No, no, no, a thousand times, no. Some of the most pathetic apologies of all talk about 'mistakes'; it is the cop-out of choice of the most craven prevaricators.

Nobody in Liverpool is ever going to forget the 1989 *Sun* front-page headline 'THE TRUTH', which made lurid allegations about the behaviour of Liverpool fans on the day of the Hillsborough tragedy. 'The coverage was a mistake . . . I made a serious error,' said Editor Kelvin McKenzie in a radio interview three months later. Not good enough. It was 'an awful error', conceded a *Sun* editorial in 2004. Still not good enough. It was 'the worst mistake in our history', admitted the paper's managing editor in 2005. They *still* hadn't got it. Where is the acknowledgement that they had not made a mistake, but acted like total shits? No wonder so many people in Liverpool still refuse to buy the paper.

More recently, in 2009, the rugby world was rocked to its foundations when a Harlequins' player, at the instigation of his coach, Dean Richards, was found to have faked a blood injury in order to get himself substituted. All hell broke loose and Richards was forced to resign. Cue an open letter of apology to Harlequins' fans from club CEO Mark Evans. After apologising for the episode, Evans added:

> 'One mistake, albeit extremely high profile, should not overshadow a career in which so much has been achieved.'

A high-profile mistake? The blood capsule used to fake the injury had been bought in a South London joke shop for the specific purpose for which it was used. So where was the mistake? Had the shopper meant to buy a whoopee cushion? Or a fake moustache? I am sure I was not alone in wanting to deposit Evans at the bottom of a Harlequins' scrum and leave him there.

Another weasel word, to be distrusted on sight, is 'regrettable'. American swimmer Michael Phelps won eight gold medals at the Beijing Olympics, but the following year, when he was forced to apologise after a photograph of him apparently smoking pot appeared in the *News of the World*, his faltering effort was not even worthy of bronze:

> 'I engaged in behaviour which was regrettable and demonstrated bad judgement . . . I acted in an inappropriate way, not in a manner that people have come to expect of me. For that, I am sorry.'

Through the veneer of contrition, one can detect the annoyance of a man whose only real regret was that he was caught.

Watered-down apologies tend to be not just weak in tone, but ridiculously long: rambling expressions of regret filled with so many subordinate clauses and qualifying epithets that you are left wondering if the lawyer who drafted them is being paid by the word. The apologisers have lost sight of the original offence; any contrition they may have felt has long since faded, and all that matters to them is couching their statement of apology in such a way that nobody can object to it, because it covers all the angles.

Here is a textbook case of the long-winded, lawyerly apology by lawyer-turned-politician Tony Blair, made while addressing the Labour Party conference in September 2004:

> 'The evidence about Saddam having actual biological and chemical weapons, as opposed to the capacity to develop them, has turned out to be wrong. I acknowledge that and accept that . . . I can apologise for the information that turned out to be wrong, but I cannot, sincerely at least, apologise for removing Saddam.'

Read it once and you think, 'Well, it's not much of an apology, but at least it's an apology.' Read it twice and you think: 'The slippery bastard. He's apologised for diddly squat.'

6. Syntactical Confidence Tricks

'Sorry' is such a sonorous, eye-catching word that it tends to obscure the words around it, but those subordinate words can be just as important in the context of the whole apology. I have already highlighted the often-overlooked distinction between being sorry *about* something and sorry *for* something, but that is just the tip of the syntactical iceberg. For someone keen to sound apologetic, while not actually admitting they have done anything wrong, the English language offers an almost limitless number of escape clauses.

Listen to this grotesquely maladroit effort by former Labour minister Margaret Beckett, who had to face the music on BBC's *Question Time* at the height of the expenses scandal. Challenged about claiming for hanging baskets and pot plants, the best she could manage was:

'That was a mistake. It should not have been made.'

I have already deplored the use of the word 'mistake' to excuse more serious wrongdoings, but this is the ultimate absurdity: the mistake that has no author because of the use of the passive tense.

Beckett should have heeded the lesson of President Reagan, whose reputation for straight talking plummeted during the Iran-Contra affair, when he tried to get away with lily-livered apologies like this:

'It's obvious that the execution of these policies was flawed and mistakes were made.'

Yes, Mr President, but *whose* mistakes were they? The passive tense was like a red rag to the bull of public opinion.

Syntactical legerdemain is the stock-in-trade of the apologiser under duress: someone who would rather not be apologising at all. When England cricket captain Mike Gatting was forced to grovel to Pakistani umpire Shakoor Rana after their infamous bust-up in Faisalabad, in 1987, his one-sentence letter of apology positively radiated his lack of contrition:

Dear Shakoor Rana,
I apologise for the bad language used during the second day of the
Test match.
Mike Gatting

The use of the passive tense is a complete fudge. Gatting might be apologising for bad language used by someone else: one of the other players, Shakoor Rana himself, even someone in the crowd.

I am sorry to keep picking on Boris Johnson, but here he is again, in 2008, apologising for allegedly racist articles which appeared in the *Spectator* when he was editor of the magazine:

'I'm sorry for what was previously written, as it does not reflect what is in my heart.'

There is some excuse for the use of the passive tense on this occasion, in that Johnson was apologising for an article written by one of his columnists, Taki, not by himself, but the wording is still weak and unsatisfactory: it does not hit the contrite note needed. And should politicians discuss the contents of their hearts, or are they inviting ridicule? It is a moot point.

One of the most egregious pieces of tense-hopping in modern politics occurred in 1997 when Tony Blair, early on in his premiership, had to grovel over the Bernie Ecclestone affair. The Formula One boss, it will be remembered, had donated £1 million to the Labour Party, then successfully lobbied the government to water down its promised ban on tobacco advertising. This was the famous interview in which Blair gave us all a good laugh by describing himself as 'a pretty straight sort of guy'. His chosen form of apology was equally risible:

'It hasn't been handled well, and for that I take full responsibility and apologise for that. I suppose what I would say to you is that perhaps I didn't focus on this and the seriousness of it the way that I should, because I was focusing on other issues.'

This, of course, is a textbook example of my first deadly sin of apologising – the apology that doubles as an excuse, and a pretty lame excuse at that. But the really objectionable thing here is the opening words: 'It hasn't been handled well' – as if someone other than the prime minister was responsible for the handling.

If the use of the passive tense is always a give-away, there are plenty of other syntactical tricks deployed by apologisers who are not genuinely apologetic and want to get away with doing the bare minimum. Watch out for that small but perfectly formed weasel word 'may', as in the oft-heard refrain: 'We apologise unreservedly to anybody we may have offended.' The little 'may', muttered so softly you can hardly hear it, turns a proper apology into a conditional one, which is largely meaningless.

Here is comedian Alan Carr backtracking frantically after an off-colour joke at the 2008 British Comedy Awards. In a gag about Karen Matthews, the Dewsbury mother convicted of kidnapping her own daughter, Carr had referred to Matthews as 'a gay icon', adding: 'People like a bit of rough, don't they?' His subsequent apology was unconvincing, to say the least:

'I realise what I said was insensitive and I am sorry for any offence this may have caused.'

The 'may' weakens the entire sentence – to the point where you are left wondering whether the comedian appreciates quite how insensitive his comments were.

7. The Token Apology

This type of apology is arguably the worst of the lot. It should never enter the public domain in the first place: it is just hot air, a misguided attempt at appeasement. You have upset someone – or someone *says* you have upset them, which is not the same thing – so you say sorry upon instinct, before you have even examined your conscience and decided whether or not you have done anything wrong. If you are not at fault, you should not be apologising, clearly. But clarity tends to get lost in the clamour of complaint.

Suppose you ring someone who happens to be having a bath at the time. From their point of view, the timing of your call is infuriating; they have to leap out of the bath, grab a towel and slither across the floor to the phone, tripping over the cat in the process. But if they snap your head off for getting them out of the bath, should you apologise? Of course not. You just politely point out the bleeding obvious – that you are not psychic.

Yet an extraordinary number of people – and I am as guilty as anyone – do apologise in that sort of situation. They think saying sorry will placate the other person. Maybe it will – but only at the cost of encouraging them to make still more outlandish complaints next time.

In wording, a token apology is similar to a watered-down apology, but its emotional genesis is different. The former stems from someone underestimating their own culpability, the latter from them *over*estimating it.

Here is a token apology of unusual ridiculousness from the BBC – or it would be unusually ridiculous if the BBC, serial capitulator at the first whiff of protest, were not responsible. In October 2009, there had been a light-hearted debate about politicians' favourite biscuits, which lured Andrew Neil, presenter of *This Week*, the late-night politics show on BBC1, into a reckless attempt at satire, likening his guests, Michael Portillo and Diane Abbot, to a custard cream and a chocolate HobNob, respectively. As Diane Abbot is black, all hell broke loose or, more accurately, there was a small number of complaints, to which the BBC reacted as if World War III had broken out, removing the joke from its website and issuing a statement through a spokesman:

'A few viewers have expressed concern that this might have been a reference to race. This was certainly not the case and the show wishes to reassure them on this point and apologise if any unintentional offence was caused.'

Presumably the BBC spokesman who ran up the white flag calculated that the apology was so innocuously worded that there was no harm in making it – better safe than sorry. But there is harm in capitulating to people who make fatuous complaints: you legitimise their lopsided view of the world at the expense of the silent, sensible majority.

This 2008 apology from Tayside Police is so comically craven that it belongs in a satirical novel. The force had decided to distribute cards in shops and pubs advertising a new non-emergency telephone number. The cards featured a trainee police dog called Rebel, a six-month-old German shepherd puppy. Unfortunately, some Muslim shopkeepers refused to display the cards, complaining that, according to some Islamic scholars, dogs were unclean. At which point, Tayside Police simply rolled over, like so many contrite puppies:

'We did not seek advice from the Force's diversity adviser before publishing and distributing the postcards. That was an oversight and we apologise for any offence caused.'

Dog-haters 1, Dog-lovers 0. What conceivable good can be achieved by fawning apologies of this type? They may placate a tiny, unrepresentative minority, but at what long-term cost? This book is not the place to discuss race relations in contemporary Britain, but it is surely worth pleading, *en passant*, for a little more common sense from people in authority. Apologising when there is no good cause to apologise only aggravates a situation.

A sub-species of the token apology, and every bit as irritating, is the trivial apology: someone apologising meticulously for a minuscule error while refusing to acknowledge far more serious wrongdoing.

The Chinese government is normally so deaf to criticism that when it was reported that the prime minister, Wen Jiabao, had made a public apology, in October 2009, it took everyone by surprise. Alas, the apology, praised for its humility in the state-run Chinese media, was so footling that it was hard to know whether to laugh or cry. In a speech to schoolchildren in Beijing, the Chinese Premier had been quoted as saying that the categories of petrology were 'sedimentary, igneous and volcanic rock'. This should have been 'sedimentary, igneous and metamorphic', he said in a letter of correction to a newspaper, apologising to readers. And very gracious of him, too; you cannot have schoolchildren getting volcanic and metamorphic rock confused. Any chance of a follow-up apology for human rights abuses in his country?

7

kill all the lawyers!

I have taken so many side swipes at lawyers in this book that now might be a good moment to tackle the profession head-on, and try to explain why I hold lawyers collectively responsible for the proliferation of apologies that insult the intelligence and dampen the spirits.

Some of my best friends are lawyers and, if you confine your dealings with them to playing golf, going to the theatre or downing prodigious quantities of chardonnay while holding maudlin conversations about sex circa 1977, they are terrific company. But let them within a hundred yards of an apology and they go haywire.

I have a barrister friend whom I will call Q, which I trust is a sufficiently cunning alias to circumvent British libel laws. Last February, Q was looking so revoltingly tanned and fit that I surmised he had been to the Caribbean.

'Not the Caribbean,' he chortled. 'The Maldives. One of my clients has decided to appeal.'

'Is that wise?'

'Of course it's not wise. But it will be lucrative. I spent three hours yesterday afternoon re-drafting their original apology.'

Nice work if you can get it.

Heaven only knows what the apology looked like by the time it had been given a face-lift. If a celebrity has got into hot water and has consulted a PR adviser about how best to rehabilitate themselves with the public, you will not be able to detect that in their public utterances. PR advisers work in the shadows: they make themselves invisible. But if the celebrity has consulted a lawyer before issuing an apology, the lawyer's fingerprints will be all over it. You may not see the lawyer, but you will see their handiwork: their almost wilful determination to turn the language of Shakespeare and Dickens into a linguistic rubbish tip.

The law as an institution is not deaf to the language of contrition. If you have been found guilty of, say, causing death by careless driving, and you can convince the court that you are genuinely remorseful, sentencing guidelines enable courts to take that remorse into account. If a newspaper is being sued for libel, it can save itself and the claimant the cost of a trial by making an appropriate apology. But practitioners of the law are another matter. High ideals of justice are undermined by an institutional failure of communication. No other professional cadre, not even Members of Parliament, has lost touch so badly with the people it is supposed to serve.

Some human beings are lawyers, necessarily, but not all lawyers are human beings. The most objectionable thing about the language used by lawyers – and, behind the language, the mind-set of lawyers – is the way it dehumanises what should be a simple human process. Straight talking goes out of the window because the lawyer is always thinking a move ahead, making contingency plans. That is particularly true when it comes to apologising. Suppose an apology backfires, worries the lawyer? Better slip in a caveat. Suppose someone sues? Better slip in twenty caveats. The legal mind is timid, pusillanimous – qualities you simply cannot afford when you are saying sorry.

A couple of years ago, I was driving through Swindon when I lost concentration momentarily and drove into the car in front. Luckily, nobody was hurt, but I still did the natural, instinctive thing, which was to say sorry to the other driver. We exchanged addresses, and the next day I wrote to him, reiterating my apology and giving him details of my insurers. Then I got on the phone to the insurers to explain what had happened. A young man listened to my story and made a note of the details.

'What did you say to the other driver?' he asked, with a note of anxiety in his voice. Well, obviously, I apologised, I said. The accident was my fault. In fact, I had sent him a letter of apology. There was such a long, shocked pause at the other end of the line that I thought the man must have fainted. 'A *letter*?' he stammered eventually. 'Did you keep a copy?'

I am not blaming him, and I am sincerely sorry if he feels offended. He was just doing his job, which was to be miserly with company funds. But the episode was symptomatic of our liability-avoiding culture: as soon as money is involved, or might be involved, people stop accepting responsibility for their actions and think purely in terms of damage limitation. What is the minimum apology they can get away with? They calculate the cost of saying sorry, but not the cost to their reputation of not saying sorry. They turn into bean-counters.

A falls foul of B for some reason, decides to apologise, then stops dead in his tracks. *What if B sues? What if my apology is taken as an admission of guilt and used against me in court? What if I am taken to the cleaners?* Natural human instincts are engulfed by neurosis. Penny-pinching undermines penitence. The apology is still-born, or barely recognisable as an apology at all. Fear of litigation dictates the entire script – and the script reads as gobbledegook as result.

In the case of, say, a multi-national chemical company accused of dumping toxic waste close to a fishing village, such legal caution is not just understandable but justified. The same applies to politicians accused of starting wars, local authorities accused

of neglecting children, or hospitals accused of lax hygiene prac-
tices. Serious charges require serious responses, studiously worded,
accurate in every particular. There is no place in them for a shaggy
dog of a word like 'sorry'. Any apologising needs to be done by a
professional.

But why does that institutional defensiveness, the fear of costly
lawsuits, have to infect the entire body politic, and bowdlerise the
language used in simple everyday apologies?

Here is a small, relatively innocuous, example of what I am talking
about.

During the 2006 Masters, Tiger Woods told an interviewer that he
had putted 'like a spaz' – short for 'spastic'. There were the inevitable protests from charities for the disabled, quickly followed by this
statement, released by a spokesman for the golfer:

'Tiger meant nothing derogatory to any person or persons and
apologises for any offence caused.'

It is the legal formulation 'person or persons' that bothers me here.
You would not hear the phrase in ordinary conversation from one
end of the year to the next; it belongs in the Disabled Persons
(Miscellaneous Provisions) (Number 2) Regulations or some other
legal text. Lawyers use it in a specific context for a specific purpose,
and to import it into a simple apology of this kind has a sanitising,
even chilling, effect. Was Woods genuinely contrite? It was impossible to tell through the fustian language.

Consult a lawyer before apologising, if you must, *but don't let
the world see that you have consulted a lawyer.* Purge your apology of
lawyer-speak, down to the last 'good faith' and 'unreservedly'. Take
out any Latin. Zap all the conditional clauses. Lose the pleas in mitigation. Last, but not least, make sure your lawyer is a hundred miles

away, tied up in a business meeting, when you deliver the apology. Otherwise, it will just reek of calculation and insincerity.

In the letter from Andy Burnham to Shami Chakrabarti that I quoted in the last chapter, there is a clanger in the very first sentence, which I have italicised for convenience:

'The very last thing I set out to do was to cause any personal offence to you, your family *or any other party*.'

In ordinary conversation, nobody uses 'party' in that sense. A party is when you get pissed or a collective term for Liberal Democrats. A normal person would simply say 'or anyone else'; it is only lawyers who use these stilted expressions. The legal jargon erects a barrier between the apologiser and the recipient of the apology. It destroys spontaneity. It nullifies feelings. It turns normal, everyday human discourse into meaningless posturing.

Sometimes it is just a single word that gives the game away. In May 2004, after the *Daily Mirror* had caused outrage by publishing photographs of soldiers of the Queen's Lancashire Regiment apparently abusing Iraqi civilians – photos that turned out to be fakes and forced Editor Piers Morgan to resign – the paper printed this apology:

'The *Daily Mirror* apologises unreservedly for publishing the pictures and deeply regrets the reputational damage done to the Queen's Lancashire Regiment and the Army in Iraq.'

Unless your dictionary is bigger than my dictionary, you will not find the word 'reputational' in it. Of course, the meaning is clear enough in context, and a pedant would probably say I was being pedantic, but someone apologising, pleading for forgiveness, trying to convince the world that they are contrite and have realised the error of their ways, cannot afford to fall back on pedantry. Saying sorry is far too important to be dressed up in important-sounding words. It is an emotional journey, not a legal process.

Reputational damage? You can almost hear the sneers of *Mirror* readers in Preston and Blackburn as their eyes fell on the phrase. If the drafters of the apology had focused on the people offended by the publication of the pictures – the soldiers of the Queen's Lancashire Regiment, doing a dirty job in Iraq, and their families, waiting anxiously at home – they might have made a better fist of it. Instead, like the men in suits who draft apologies at the BBC, or in Downing Street, or in the legal departments of big American corporations, they were working in a bubble of their own making, cut off from normal human feelings. That should, of course, read 'people in suits' – I apologise for any inadvertent offence caused.

In the 1988 movie *A Fish Called Wanda*, John Cleese, who plays an English barrister, is forced to say sorry to the baddie, played by Kevin Kline. 'Apologise!' screams Kline, after Cleese has called him a vulgarian. Cleese refuses, so Kline suspends him out of a third-floor window by his ankles. Cleese hastily apologises, upside down, reeling off all the time-honoured clichés of his profession:

> 'I apologise unreservedly . . . I offer a complete and utter retraction. The imputation was totally without basis in fact and was motivated purely by malice, and I deeply regret any distress that my comments may have caused to you or your family, and I hereby undertake not to repeat any such slander at any time in the future.'

It is a delicious scene, and it works because we all recognise, only too well, the kind of legal mumbo-jumbo the film is satirising. But that doesn't stop us using the mumbo-jumbo ourselves, and using it more and more.

The legal mind-set is pervasive. Professional lawyers may only account for a tiny fraction of the population, but their pernickety habits of thought have infected the rest of us. We think long words are better than short words. We fixate on worst-case scenarios. We are convinced that using the word 'sorry' will cost us money – which, in the real world, is very seldom the case. In fact, many apologies actually *save* money, by taking the sting out of a situation.

A 2009 research study at Nottingham University illustrated this point to perfection. The study found that companies that apologise to disgruntled customers are likely to achieve significantly better results than companies that offer financial compensation in lieu of an apology. Researchers worked with a company responsible for sales on eBay, and tested two alternative consumer-relations strategies on customers who had put negative feedback on the eBay website. The first strategy entailed offering customers a simple apology and asking them to remove their comments from the site; the second entailed making no apology, but offering customers a small financial sweetener, of a few euros, if they withdrew their comments.

Far more customers – 45 per cent compared with 23 per cent – were wooed by the first strategy than the second. All they had got was a few soothing words, drafted by someone they had never met, but those words, seemingly, meant more to them than money.

The obvious conclusion to be drawn from the research, if one is being cynical, is that talk is cheap. We have become so accustomed to using the s-word indiscriminately that we accept apologies equally indiscriminately, opting for the quiet life at all costs. But I think there is another, less cynical, conclusion, too.

People bicker, fall out, have their differences, swear, shout, call each other every name under the sun, but they don't want those differences to fester and fester until they end up in court. Their anger burns itself out. Give them the briefest glimpse of an olive branch and they will grab it. Show a little consideration of their feelings and they will react with relief and gratitude. It is lawyers, and those who put their trust in lawyers, who try to spin out disputes out for as long as possible, arguing the toss, refusing to back down.

They have made 'sorry' a dirty word – which is such a wanton perversion of language that someone should sue them.

8

right on the money

After all the verbal train crashes in the preceding chapters, it is tempting to conclude that every apology is doomed to fail, or not fully succeed. In fact, there have been some wonderful apologies over the years, ones that were so pitch-perfect, rooted in such genuine humility, that they have actually enhanced the reputation of the person who was out of order in the first place.

Hugh Grant facing the music after the Divine Brown episode

Hugh Grant is now such a well-established actor that it is easy to forget how close his career came to being derailed in 1995. The Englishman was about to launch his Hollywood career in the movie *Nine Months* when he was caught by Los Angeles police engaged in a sexual act with a prostitute, Divine Brown. The humiliating photograph of Grant in police custody made front pages all over the world, but, instead of lying low, the actor continued with his schedule of chat-show appearances, turning them to his advantage with the disarmingly frank way in which he said sorry.

On *Larry King Live*, he said:

'I could accept some of the things that people have explained: stress, pressure, loneliness, that that was the reason. But that would be false. In the end, you have to come clean and say, "I did something dishonourable, shabby and goatish."'

If that was right on the money, his interview with Jay Leno went one better. Of the Divine Brown episode, Grant said simply:

'I think you know in life what's a good thing to do and what's a bad thing, and I did a bad thing, and there you have it.'

What an exhilarating contrast to the convoluted lawyer-speak of most celebrity apologies! You would have to trawl the works of Shakespeare and Dickens to find another sentence of twenty-eight words in which every word hits the mark and every word is a monosyllable.

Andrew Hawkins apologising for his ancestor's part in the slave trade

Politicians in two hemispheres have fallen over themselves to say sorry for the slave trade, but none of their stage-managed public apologies made as much impact as the bold, heartfelt gesture by Cornishman Andrew Hawkins.

In 2006, when Hawkins discovered that one of his ancestors, Sir John Hawkins, a famous sixteenth-century shipbuilder, had also been a slave-trader, he travelled to West Africa to express his contrition in person. Kneeling in chains before a large crowd in the Gambia, at the International Roots Festival, Hawkins said that, as a member of the Hawkins family, he did not accept that what happened was right, and went on:

'The slave trade was an abomination to God and I have come to ask the African people for their forgiveness.'

Just a stunt, cynics would say. What good could such an apology possibly achieve, four centuries after the event? But if it was a stunt, it was a stunt that took rare courage. Hawkins, remember, had absolutely no way of knowing how his gesture would be received by his African audience; he risked being ridiculed and publicly humiliated. Only when there was a flutter of applause did he know that his apology had been taken in the spirit in which it was intended. The episode underscored the element of danger attached to apologising: it is not easy; the outcome is not guaranteed; but there is a rich emotional dividend if you can pull it off.

Francis Bacon apologising to a parliamentary committee in 1621

Francis Bacon may not have written the plays of Shakespeare, as some have argued, but the seventeenth-century statesman was no slouch with words, as he demonstrated at the nadir of his career when he was charged with corruption as Lord Chancellor and arraigned before a parliamentary committee. Asked if a confession he had signed was true, Bacon said simply:

'My lords, it is my act, my hand and my heart; I beseech your lordships to be merciful.'

Compared with the equivocal, blustering apologies of MPs caught up in the expenses scandal, the choice of words has a lapidary elegance.

John Lennon apologising for
claiming the Beatles were bigger than Jesus

He rambled, he was on the defensive, he looked ill at ease, he was not remotely contrite, but there was still something oddly engaging, a loucheness under fire, in the apology John Lennon delivered at a press conference in Chicago in 1966, after his much-quoted comment 'we're more popular than Jesus' outraged Christians in the United States:

> 'I wasn't saying whatever they said I was saying. I'm sorry I said it really. I never meant it to be a lousy anti-religious thing. I apologise if that will make you happy. I still don't know quite what I've done. I've tried to tell you what I did do, but if you want me to apologise, if that will make you happy, then I'm sorry.'

Not one for the purists, certainly; in fact, it breaks almost all the rules of apologising, with its grudging conditional clauses and its mixed messages. I still like the balance of it, though; the sly irony, proffering the s-word while, at the same time, gently questioning the sanity of the people demanding the apology.

There was an amusing postscript to the Lennon apology more than forty years later when the Vatican signalled its acceptance of the apology. A 2008 article in *L'Osservatore Romano*, the official Vatican newspaper, declared that the Beatle had been guilty of nothing more than: 'a boast by a young working-class Englishman, faced with unexpected success, after growing up in the legend of Elvis Presley and rock and roll.' It is a shame Lennon was not alive to read the article. He would have found the subtext – no middle- or upper-class Englishman could possibly have made the same error – quite hilarious.

Winston Churchill making a gracious exit from prison

There is always something rather touching in a handsome apology that is totally uncalled-for. One of the most celebrated episodes of Winston Churchill's early years was his capture and imprisonment while serving as a war correspondent during the Second Boer War. He escaped from prison, but not before he had left a letter to Louis de Souza, the Boer Secretary of War, on his pillow:

> 'I have the honour to inform you that as I do not consider that your government has any right to detain me as a military prisoner, I have decided to escape from your custody . . . Regretting that I am unable to bid you a more ceremonious or a personal farewell, I have the honour to be, Sir, your most obedient servant, Winston Churchill.'

The writer's tongue is firmly in his cheek, but by keeping the veneer of good manners, he retains the moral high ground with aplomb.

Brigadier General Mark Kimmit
putting his president to shame

Plain talking is one of the soldierly virtues, and it can be seen at its best in this 2004 apology by Brigadier General Mark Kimmit, then US Deputy Director of Operations in Iraq, after photographs of American soldiers abusing Iraqi detainees in Abu Ghraib prison caused worldwide condemnation. In Washington, President Bush was still prevaricating, hedging his bets; he made no direct apology to the victims of the abuse. In Baghdad, addressing the Iraqi media, Kimmit was not so reticent. He cut straight to the chase:

'My army has been embarrassed by this. My army has been shamed by this. And on behalf of my army, I apologise for what those soldiers did to your citizens.'

Try putting the same words into the mouth of President Bush, with 'country' substituted for 'Army'. It is impossible. There is nothing a politician hates more than issuing an unqualified apology – even when only an unqualified apology will satisfy public opinion. Serving soldiers are not so pig-headed; they know when to beat a dignified retreat.

André Hanscombe apologising to the man he thought had murdered his girlfriend

The stabbing of Rachel Nickell on Wimbledon Common in 1992 was one of the most brutal murders of modern times. For her partner, André Hanscombe, it was particularly harrowing. All his anger was directed at the prime suspect, Colin Stagg, and even after Stagg had been acquitted at his trial at the Old Bailey, he pursued his vendetta against him, calling him a liar and demanding a retrial. Most of us would probably have felt the same in his shoes, but in 2009, after Stagg's innocence had finally been established and another man convicted of the crime, Hanscombe sent him a touchingly contrite letter:

'Dear Colin, I am very sorry for the ordeal you have endured during this very sad affair, and any part that I might have had personally to make it worse . . . I now know that you were, and are, an innocent man who was mistakenly charged. I wish you a long, happy and productive life.'

Generous sentiments, and Stagg responded in kind: 'It was a really kind gesture, and I know how difficult it must have been for him to make . . . I accept his apology with gratitude. It means a lot to me.'

Mark Twain grovelling to the First Lady

Husbands who accept social invitations without first getting the go-ahead from their wives are playing with fire at the best at the times. When it happened to Mark Twain in 1887, he realised that, having accepted an invitation from Mrs Grover Cleveland, the First Lady, he had a prior engagement at home. His subsequent letter of apology is a fine example of penitence unconfined. It concludes:

'I have been not only sorry but very sincerely ashamed of having made an engagement to go without first making sure that I could keep it, and I do not know how to apologise enough for my heedless breech of good manners.'

How could anyone fail to respond positively to such an unstinting show of contrition? So many written apologies just sound embarrassed, frigid: this one has real human warmth.

David Beckham apologising to the nation
after getting sent off in the 1998 World Cup

Football fans will have no difficulty remembering the low point in David Beckham's career, when he was sent off during the 1998 World Cup after kicking out at an Argentinian opponent. The headline in the *Daily Mirror* the following morning – 'TEN HEROIC LIONS, ONE STUPID BOY' – became a classic. Less well remembered is the handsome apology Beckham issued the next day:

113

'I have apologised to the England players and management, and I want every English supporter to know how deeply sorry I am.'

Simple, unambiguous, word perfect, with that little 'deeply' underscoring the apology to perfect effect; you cannot fault the sentence in any way – and this from a man whose mangled English syntax ('We was well beaten on the night') has made him a laughing stock among the intelligentsia. That is the beauty, and the challenge, of the s-word. You do not need to be clever to use it well: you just need to have the necessary humility. How many other millionaire footballers in similar circumstances have blustered, prevaricated, made excuses, blamed the referee, wallowed in self-pity or gone to ridiculous lengths to avoid accepting responsibility for their actions?

Taiwanese President Ma Ying-jeou apologising for the failures of his government in the wake of Typhoon Morakat

Earlier in the book, I took President Bush to task for his belated, and wretchedly inadequate, apology for the failures of his administration in the wake of Hurricane Katrina. It is worth contrasting his performance with the public apology issued by President Ma Ying-jeou of Taiwan in not dissimilar circumstances. After Taiwan was devastated by Typhoon Morakat in 2009, and the government was heavily criticised for its inadequate response, President Ma appeared on television with his most senior ministers and made the following statement:

'As national leader, I must accept responsibility for all of the mistakes made by the government during the disaster rescue work. I wish to express my deepest apology to all of the people, especially to persons whose relatives died or disappeared.'

After making his statement, President Ma and his ministers abased themselves, literally, by bowing from the waist in a gesture of contrition and holding the position for thirty seconds. What chance of errant Western politicians taking a leaf out the Taiwanese book? The theatrical choreography would not work in Washington or Westminster (too many ministers would have to display gaping bald patches) but it is worth noting the obvious moral: *better an over-the-top apology than a mealy-mouthed one.*

Tom Hanks retracting offensive comments about the Mormons

Apologising to bigoted Mormons sticks in the throat, but there are times when it has to be done. In January 2009, Tom Hanks attacked the Church of Latter Day Saints for trying to amend Californian state law and ban gay marriages. He said that their proposal amounted to 'codified discrimination' and added: 'There are a lot of people who feel that is un-American, and I am one of them.' This caused such outrage in the Mormon community that the actor was forced to retract the comment, saying that while he believed the proposed Mormon amendment *did* represent codified discrimination:

'Everyone has a right to vote their conscience – nothing could be more American. No one should use "un-American" lightly or in haste. I did. I should not have.'

What I like here is not just the simple language, but the precision. A single word had given offence, and understandably, so Hanks, without giving ground on the main point of principle, apologised for his use of that word. One can think of many other members of his profession who would have obstinately stuck to their guns, thinking:

'You can't apologise to *Mormons*.' Hanks had the maturity to review his remarks objectively, in a spirit of self-criticism.

Graham Greene goes on a charm offensive

Few apologies have had such far-reaching consequences as one Graham Greene made when he was an undergraduate at Oxford in the 1920s. Having written a deliberately provocative article about sex, religion and the cinema for a student magazine, Greene received a stern letter of rebuke from one Vivien Dayrell-Browning, a Roman Catholic. Greene replied by return of post, suitably contrite:

'I most sincerely apologise. I'm afraid any excuses will seem very lame, but I wrote the article in a frightful hurry . . . At the same time, I was feeling intensely fed up with things and wanted to be as offensive as I could . . . I really am very sorry. Will you forgive me, and come and have tea with me as a sign of forgiveness?'

The rest is history. Vivien came to tea, they got married and Greene converted to Roman Catholicism. But suppose he had been too pig-headed to apologise? He might have died a Protestant and written dreary novels about middle-class adultery in Gloucestershire.

Prince William showing princely chivalry

Chivalry is at the soul of apologising, and there is nothing more heart-warming than an apology that is not just generous, but extravagant to the point of ludicrousness. In May 2009, 109-year-old Catherine Masters from Oxfordshire wrote a letter of complaint

to Buckingham Palace, grumbling that the Queen was always wearing exactly the same outfit – a yellow dress – in the birthday cards she had sent Ms Masters since she reached her centenary. Imagine her surprise when Prince William turned up in person at her nursing home to convey his grandmother's apologies and promise that in future cards the Queen would be wearing a different-coloured dress. Prince and commoner then spent forty minutes chatting over a cup of tea, discussing such arcane topics as the best way to cook shepherd's pie. It was a delightful episode, quintessentially English, and it showed how, in the right hands, apologising need not be a chore, but a positive pleasure. Any anti-monarchist pique Ms Masters may have felt was swept aside by a daringly executed charm offensive.

'Huguenot' doing the decent thing in the East Dulwich Forum

I have no idea who 'Huguenot' is, or what kind of man lurks behind the alias, but I like his style. He is one of the regular posters on the East Dulwich Forum, one of those middle-class cyber-villages that are fast putting pubs out of business. Specimen threads include *Is the N-word Necessarily Racist?*, *Bring Back the Birch*, and *Anyone Else Had the Swine Flu Jab?* The flow of ideas is vigorous, sometimes over-vigorous, hence the need for this online apology from 'Huguenot' in November 2009:

> 'I appreciate I went beyond the pale recently, and let a number of people down, exposing them to criticisms which they didn't deserve. I was both short-tempered and foolish. I was also foul-mouthed, which isn't really acceptable. I'd like to apologise, particularly to TLS and Quids. TLS for letting my irritation sway my judgement, and Quids for being a pompous ass.'

If only more public figures could apologise with the same easy grace. You don't need to know the background to the apology, just note the combination of factual precision – the apologiser clearly identifies both his own shortcomings and the individuals to whom he needs to apologise – and spontaneity of delivery. The tone is conversational, the language unforced. A smidgeon of regret, a little gentle self-flagellation and a teaspoonful of humour. It is a near-perfect recipe.

Oprah Winfrey apologising to the ex-wife of Mike Tyson

Oprah Winfrey's touchy-feely approach to TV interviews has had her admired and reviled in equal measure. But, on the odd occasions the chat-show queen has been forced to apologise, she has shown herself a master of simple, direct communication.

In November 2009, Winfrey was taken to task by Robin Givens, ex-wife of Mike Tyson, for mishandling an interview with the boxer and not treating a joke he made about wife-beating with proper seriousness. Winfrey took the criticism on the chin and apologised to Givens immediately:

> 'I would say to you and every woman who has ever been hit: I did not handle that as well as I should have, and I should have said more to clarify that what he was doing and saying was wrong . . . So I apologise to you and I apologise to every woman who has ever been in that situation.'

Imagine Jonathan Ross – or any other male chat-show host for that matter – eating humble pie so graciously, without quibbling or resorting to irony. It is well-nigh impossible.

Willy Brandt kneeling before the memorial
at the Jewish ghetto in Warsaw in 1970

In saying sorry, actions can sometimes speak louder than words. 'I did what human beings do when speech fails them,' said Willy Brandt of one of the most moving of all political apologies. Brandt, as Chancellor of West Germany, was laying a wreath at the memorial at the Jewish ghetto in Warsaw in December 1970 when, quite spontaneously, he knelt before the monument. The gesture had not been planned in advance. Brandt, who had fled to Norway before the war and took no part in Nazi atrocities, simply felt overwhelmed that, in his words, he was standing 'at the bottom of the abyss of German history, under the burden of millions of victims of murder'.

The immediate reaction was mixed. An opinion poll in Germany found that 48 per cent of people found the gesture excessive, compared with 41 per cent who thought it appropriate. But how many people now think that Brandt overdid his apology? It has stood the test of time better than a thousand more calculated expressions of remorse.

9

alan turing, the slave trade, the sack of constantinople and 101 other things we are really, really sorry for

In 2008, visitors to the Church of England website will have been amused/aghast to read the following official bicentenary apology to Charles Darwin:

'Two hundred years from your birth, the Church of England owes you an apology for misunderstanding you and, by getting our first reaction wrong, encouraging others to misunderstand you still.'

The wording is so inept it is beyond parody. There must have been Anglicans flirting with Rome, convinced the C of E was going to the dogs, who got on the phone to their nearest Catholic drop-in centre when they read this wobbly *blancmange* of PC revisionism. One can imagine the great naturalist himself not just turning in his grave, but reviewing his entire theory of evolution. On this evidence, the human species is not progressing, but regressing, and at a rate of knots. If educated Englishmen can write this sort of stuff a mere four hundred years after Shakespeare and the *Book of Common Prayer*, how long before *Homo sapiens* is crawling through swamps again, emitting nothing but grunts?

My research revealed, embarrassingly, that this apology was written by a man who was at Oxford with me, and someone I hold in warm regard. I am sincerely and unreservedly sorry if he feels offended by my comments, but he is a reasonable man and may, on reflection, concede that his choice of words was inappropriate and, with hindsight, constituted a lamentable error of judgement.

In essence, the wording just sounds tortured, as if it has been through ten drafts too many. The author has lost his innocence. I remember an occasion, back in the days when we were students together, when we bumped into each other in the college quad. He said sorry, it was his fault, I said, no, it was my fault, he said sorry again, I said sorry again and, if memory serves, we went off to the pub and said sorry long into the night. Happy days.

If the wording stinks, in its sentiments it is a very twenty-first-century apology, the kind you come across all the time. Anglicans who read the apology and converted to Rome in disgust, thinking they were joining an institution that had the courage of its convictions and did not kow-tow to dead naturalists, would have been in for a shock. Except when it comes to child abuse, the Catholic Church of the third millennium is more willing to apologise, admit its fallibility and atone for its sins than at any other time in its history. In fact, probably no one individual did more to make apologising fashionable than the late Pope John Paul II, who, in the course of his long pontificate, issued over a hundred apologies – a truly extraordinary tally, given that Popes, *ex officio*, are supposed to be infallible. It was as if John le Mesurier had been elected Supreme Pontiff.

The apologies ranged from the specific – the behaviour of Crusaders during the Sack of Constantinople in 1204 – to the general – the treatment of women through the centuries – and if they made a few non-Catholics give a wry smile, they were offered with the best of intentions. The Pope from Poland understood, better than his predecessors, the importance of humility.

The urge to put right the wrongs of the past runs very deep in modern society, which is no bad thing. We cannot rewrite history, but we can, on occasion, make public acknowledgement of the errors of our forefathers, particularly when the mistaken attitudes of the past have bequeathed a legacy of prejudice and rancour that still lingers.

At the start of the book, I looked at Gordon Brown's 2009 apology to gay code-breaker Alan Turing, and its glaring flaw – the prime minister was saying sorry for something that happened when he was one year old. To pedantically minded people, such apologies are always going to have a hollow ring: they drive a coach and horses through what should be at the heart of an apology, the acceptance of personal responsibility for past wrongdoings. But should the pedants be allowed to win this argument? Or does one need to look at the conundrum through a slightly different lens?

The treatment of Alan Turing was not just grossly unfair to him, but symptomatic of a wider social malaise: a lack of charity that infected the entire body politic. Even at its finest hour (Winston Churchill was still prime minister at the time Turing was convicted) Britain had a moral blind spot: it denied gay people their essential humanity.

Many, though not all, gay Britons gave the Turing apology a warm welcome. For them, it represented another step on the long road to emancipation. Gays may no longer be criminalised in this country, but many of them still have to run the gauntlet of hostility and prejudice. Who would want to be a gay footballer in that brutal, disrespectful world?

For the prime minister to apologise for the way Turing was treated in the 1950s was, if nothing else, a gesture of solidarity with a group of people who, in many cases, still feel beleaguered fifty years later.

For that reason alone it was probably justified, whatever the pedants say. An apology should not be a self-serving exercise, but a salve for the hurt feelings of others. And if there are people who still feel the hurt of the bigoted attitudes that led to Turing being treated as a criminal, why not acknowledge those feelings, however clumsily?

Other politicians pressed to make apologies for things that happened before they came to power, whether it happened in 1993 or 1793, should make the same kind of profit–loss calculation as Mr Brown. There is no point in getting bogged down in turgid debate about the theoretical validity of such apologies: that can be left to leader-writers with nothing better to do. As politicians, they should focus on political outcomes. Will the apology they are contemplating please more people than it displeases? Will it come across as a states-manlike gesture, consonant with the dignity of their office? Or will it just look like headline chasing? In a volatile, cynical world, those can be hard judgements to make.

As a general rule, things that have happened in the past, outside our control, are not our responsibility. To pretend that they are, and that we can somehow put past wrongs right, is at best delusional, at worst arrogant.

I have never apologised to Africans for the slave trade, Scots for the Battle of Culloden or Germans for the bombing of Dresden, but I was once moved, in a pub in Brisbane in 2002, to apologise to an Australian cricket fan for Bodyline, the tactics used by England fast bowlers during the 1932–33 tour.

The Australian had bought me four beers, I had only bought him three beers, so it seemed chivalrous to redress the balance. Our conversation went something like this. I have omitted burps, some swear words, fuddled pauses and one lengthy visit to the lavatory or, as they say in Brisbane, dunny.

Me: Bodyline was a bloody disgrace.

Australian: You're not wrong, mate.

Me: We couldn't get Don Bradman out, so we tried to hit the little bastard on the head. Not cricket.

Australian: What are you saying, mate? That it was cheating?

Me: That's *exactly* what I'm saying. Should've been a law against it.

Australian: Too bloody right there should've.

Me: An Aussie batsman could have been killed. And you know what?

Australian: What, mate?

Me: I'm really, really sorry.

Australian: That's big of you, mate.

Me: You're welcome. Bodyline sucked. Unsporting. Sorry it happened. The Poms behaved abominably, and I'm a Pom and I feel bad about it. And I want to apologise on behalf of the MCC, of which I'm a member, and the entire England cricket team. Shake hands?

The handshake went on so long we nearly fell off our bar stools. My apology was good for Anglo–Australian relations, I suppose, but how absurd I feel looking back at the incident. I made one of the classic errors of the apologiser: over-egged the pudding.

A sense of proportion is vital to apologising. Let us imagine that I have a daughter who feels passionately about the environment and blames my generation for squandering the planet's resources. I concede her point and apologise: 'Darling, you're quite right. I shouldn't have wasted so much energy. I'm sorry about that. I will buy a more fuel-efficient car and change to an eco-friendly heating system.' If I mean what I say, I will get a grateful response. But suppose I then add, 'And while I'm apologising, I would like to say sorry for all the North Sea gas wasted by the people who lived in this house before us.' Gratitude would turn to fury in an instant. 'Daddy, you're taking the piss.' I would have made a mockery of the apology by trying to amplify it beyond its natural proportions.

Politicians apologising for the slave trade and the like may not be acting quite as ridiculously as me in this hypothetical example. They are public figures, with public responsibilities; they are in a position to speak for others, in a way that I cannot. But they *are* being ridiculous, and it is important, before they embark on their journey of contrition, that they acknowledge that. They need to recognise that some people will laugh at them, and *why* those people will laugh at them, and acknowledge the legitimacy of that laughter, in the chorus of other sounds.

So what makes a public apology laughable, and therefore politically unwise? That depends, not just on the apology itself, but on the identity of the person doing the apologising. In 2007, when London mayor Ken Livingstone said sorry for the role played by London in the slave trade, most people just giggled. Was this the same Ken Livingstone who, two years previously, had refused to apologise for likening a reporter from the *Evening Standard* to a concentration-camp guard? There was a comic discrepancy between the mayor's reluctance to accept personal responsibility for his actions and his enthusiastic shouldering of responsibility for the actions of long-dead Londoners. Far from enhancing his reputation, the apology was another nail in his political coffin.

At least London had been a hub of the slave trade. When Peter Hain, Secretary of State for Wales and Northern Ireland at the time, leapt on the bandwagon, apologising for the fact that people in Belfast and Cardiff had also profited from the slave trade, he got the loud raspberry his apology deserved. As historians were quick to point out, those cities had actually played a prominent role in the abolition of slavery. A politician on the make – Hain was bidding to become deputy leader of the Labour Party at the time – stood exposed for the opportunist he was. He should have kept his mouth shut.

Few politicians of his generation have opposed racism more implacably than Hain, who first came to prominence as an anti-apartheid campaigner in the 1960s, but by rushing out an apology that was not fit for purpose, not seeing how ridiculous it would sound, he undid a lot of his good work. The Labour Party elected Harriet Harman deputy leader instead – for which someone really *should* have apologised.

With his antennae on the blink, Hain forgot one of the golden rules of apologising: *if you are apologising for something that happened in the past, then the further in the past it happened, the more ridiculous you will look.* When he was fighting apartheid, the evils he was excoriating were present and immediate. The victims of the slave trade – whatever its long-term legacy – had been in their grave for centuries, which makes any apology for the slave trade automatically meaningless, and also sets the bar higher when it comes to avoiding ridicule.

All politics is about votes, ultimately, and if an apology goes down well with a majority of voters, it can be adjudged a success. But short-term popularity can be misleading. History has vindicated Willy Brandt, whose dramatic gesture at the Jewish ghetto in Warsaw I described in the last chapter, but at the time, remember, a majority of ordinary Germans found the gesture over the top.

Australian premier Kevin Rudd, in contrast, hit the popularity jackpot in 2008, when he issued his celebrated apology to indigenous Australians. Sorry Day, as it became known, enjoyed rave reviews, with a poll in the *Sydney Morning Herald* showing 62 per cent of voters enthusiastic about the apology, compared with only 16 per cent who thought it a bad idea. Most politicians can only dream of that kind of approval rating. With his well-crafted speech, Rudd seemed to have caught the public mood to perfection, but whether the apology will stand the test of time, as Brandt's has done, is another matter. There is a paper-thin margin between a popular gesture and a populist gesture.

Given that the gravamen of the apology was the need to respect the rights of minorities, there was scant tolerance shown to the minority who questioned the need for the apology. When Brendan Nelson, the Australian Leader of the Opposition, made a matching apology, but with one or two qualifications, the crowds watching telecasts of the proceedings on big screens in Perth, Melbourne and Sydney booed so loudly that Nelson was drowned out. His speech reads pretty well on the printed page, whether you agree with it or not, but the mob had decided to say sorry and the mob was not going to listen to anyone who dared to cavil. You *had* to be sorry, in the same way that, in this country, you had to be devastated by the death of Diana. Not pretty.

Rudd meant well, but if he thought his apology would close an unhappy chapter in Australian history, he was getting ahead of himself. That chapter is still being written. The racial fault-lines in Australian society are as deep as ever.

The Australian prime minister was on stronger ground eighteen months later when he issued a second public apology, this time to the thousands of children who were deported to Australia from the United Kingdom in the middle of the last century. The children had been abandoned by their parents, so it was hoped they could start a new life in Australia – and be a source of cheap white labour when they grew up. Instead, most of the children suffered brutal abuse in their new country, while losing all family links in their old one. They had been robbed of their childhoods, as Rudd eloquently acknowledged in a speech to some of the surviving children in Canberra.

The deporting of British children to Australia stopped in 1970, when Kevin Rudd was thirteen, still a child himself. *That* gave the pedants an easy stick to beat him with: how could he apologise for policies for which he bore no responsibility? But seeing the faces of the people to whom he was apologising – most of them now well advanced in years yet still with a slightly anxious air, as if they had never fully recovered from their wretched start in life – knocked that sterile argument for six. 'You can't say sorry for a lost childhood,' said one of the deported children. 'But you can acknowledge it, and that's what I needed.' Set against that need, unanswered for years, like an undressed wound, the semantic quibbling seemed not just redundant, but offensive.

Kevin Rudd's apology was later matched by one from Gordon Brown, on behalf of the British governments who had sanctioned the deportation of the children. Again, it was well received, on the whole, because it was targeted at real people with real feelings, not historical abstractions.

Of course, the pedants remain sceptical, and in a world of strict accountability, where we each have to take personal responsibility for our actions, make the best of our lot, and not expect other people to compensate for our deficiencies, the pedants are right – 100 per cent right, as the pedants would be quick to point out. But is strict accountability in such matters the only true morality? Isn't there room for a kind of morality in which soothing the hurt feelings of other people is good in itself, quite regardless of notions of accountability?

More generally, should we welcome or deplore this type of apology? Look forward to more knee-bending to victims of historic injustices? Or view the whole trend with unalloyed cynicism? Having set myself up as an expert on saying sorry, I should be able to reach a firm conclusion on the question, which is likely to arise more and more, if the apology industry expands at its present rate. But, to be honest, I find it quite impossible.

If I were a Downing Street policy adviser, and the prime minister of the day were contemplating making an apology for something that happened in the 1950s, my advice would be very simple: 'Just do your sums, Prime Minister. Make an educated guess at the number of people who will feel better because of your apology. Now make an educated guess at the number of people who will be wetting themselves with laughter. If the first number is bigger than the second number, apologise. If it is lower, keep schtum.' But is it quite that simple? Can questions of state be reduced to a mathematical formula?

This is just not an area where I feel happy making generalisations. I am split down the middle as to whether these apologies do more harm than good. Some of them make me laugh out loud, they are so preposterous. Wasn't there a Danish minister recently who apologised to the Irish because the Vikings had raped their womenfolk? Or did I dream that? Others give me a little surge of pleasure. I feel a lump in the throat. I well up with tears I cannot explain. I think: 'I'm *glad* they said that. Someone should have said sorry years ago.' The apologies hit the spot, but then I start to have second thoughts. Did they really hit the spot? Or was I just ambushed by sentimentality?

I am sorry to be so indecisive. I really am.

10

towards an etiquette of apologising

So where does that leave us? If apologising is so problem-strewn, and 'sorry' one of the slipperiest words in the language, maddeningly imprecise, why not just abandon the struggle, forget grovelling and live with the consequences?

Earlier in the book, I took Sir Alex Ferguson to task for a mealy-mouthed, out-of-character apology. The Scot would no doubt retort, after an expletive or two: 'Exactly. That's why I don't believe in apologising. You can't please people. I didn't get where I am today by saying sorry every time I upset someone. I just get on with my job, which is managing a football club, not running a prayer meeting.' And a lot of people, even those who dislike the man, would probably share his sentiments.

If a refusal to apologise can sometimes be symptomatic of arrogance, there are other times when it can be courageous, even heroic, not to say sorry. In a different kind of book one could celebrate some of the men and women who, even under intense pressure, stuck to their guns rather than trotting out a ritual apology to keep other people happy.

Take cricketer Harold Larwood. After the infamous Bodyline tour to Australia in 1932–3, the MCC tried to make a scapegoat of the

Nottinghamshire fast bowler, demanding that he apologise for his part in the tour. Larwood treated the demand with the contempt it deserved. He never played for England again, but he had kept his integrity.

So, yes, there are good arguments against the promotion of sorry-saying as a way of life – good for the soul, and all that. Modern life unfolds at breakneck speed, there is no time for introspection, navel-gazing, interminable post-mortems – people want to move on. Even sensitive souls who hate hurting anyone, and feel mortified when they do, rarely have time to mend fences properly, down the last paling: they just have to stammer their apologies and hope for the best.

Saying sorry may have become a national craze – and demanding apologies of others even more of a craze, a bit of light entertainment to fill the time between *Strictly Come Dancing* and *The X Factor* – but there is also a long tradition in this country of viewing apologies as otiose and excessive. They are messy. They are problematic. They involve public displays of emotion, which goes against the grain of the national character.

That is probably why some of the people who have been most suspicious of apologising are also people one thinks of as quintes-sentially English.

'It is a good rule in life never to apologise,' said P.G. Wodehouse, creator of that inveterate crawler Bertie Wooster, forever appeasing his aunts. 'The right sort of people do not want apologies; and the wrong sort take mean advantage of them.' Wodehouse was not being snobbish – unlike Tory grandee Alan Clark, when he sneered: 'Only domestic servants apologise for things they have said.' He was simply reflecting on the folly of thinking that things can be put right by a few mumbled words of contrition.

They seldom can – as nobody knew better than Wodehouse. His own life pivoted on his catastrophically ill-judged decision to do radio broadcasts from Berlin during the war, after he had been interned by the Nazis. He could have apologised a million times for 'a grave error of judgement, for which I am unreservedly sorry', but nobody would have listened to him, not while feelings were running so high. Only time was able to heal the wound.

But just because apologies cannot always deliver instant results does not make them redundant. If you have messed up and want to get your life back on track, with your reputation restored, you have to start somewhere.

The s word alone is not enough, but it is a necessary first step on the road to redemption – assuming you want redemption, which, deep down, and whatever name you give it, we all do. Of course, excessive apologising – to which I have already pleaded guilty – can be pretty irritating. Somewhere, deep in my memory bank, is a female voice raised in anger: 'Max, why do you keep saying *sorry* the whole time?' I have forgotten who it was – I am sorry about that, I should be able to remember her name. But I can hear her voice very clearly: it was deep, almost husky, with a slight American twang. Alison? Angela? Antonia? And I remember her stamping her foot in irritation as she delivered the line. It was a warning shot, and perhaps I should have taken her distaste for apologetic men more seriously than I did. I imagine she is married to a banker now.

But, warning shots or no warning shots, I have never been able to kick the apology habit. If anything, I now say sorry more than ever – and I have no intention of apologising for that.

It all comes down to simple arithmetic. Whenever I do this equation – and I urge readers to do the same – I come up with the same answer: *If X is the number of people to whom I wish I had said sorry, but didn't, and Y is the number of people to whom I have said sorry, but wish I hadn't, then X is greater than Y.* In fact, X is so much greater than Y that it is a wonder I don't draw the obvious conclusion, pick up the phone tomorrow and start making all those apologies I should have made years ago.

My calculations are not error-proof, I concede that; there are probably people to whom I have apologised who have accepted my apology but thought: 'Call that an apology? You're *pathetic*.' But even allowing for a margin of error, the facts speak for themselves, at least, as far as my life is concerned: saying sorry has worked.

Here is another simple arithmetical proposition that works for me and, I can guarantee, will work for you too. *If X is the number of people who have apologised to me in good faith, and whose apologies I have accepted, and Y is the number of people who have apologised to me in good faith, and whose apologies I have rejected, then X is greater than Y.* Again, X is not just greater than Y, but overwhelmingly greater. In fact, I cannot think of a single sincere apology that I have greeted with anything less than gratitude and relief. And if I am grateful for their apologies, why would they not be grateful for my apologies? In the jungle of life, we all need to scratch each other's backs from time to time.

That is why I have no truck with the rednecks who say: 'Let's stop this sorry malarkey. It has got completely out of hand. We can't go around apologising to anyone and everyone.' They are plain wrong. They have not looked at the issue straight. They have ignored the most important evidence of all – the evidence of their own hearts.

Sorry may be the hardest word, but it can also be one of the healthiest, according to American scientists. The scientists measured the blood pressure of a group of women during an experiment in which they were abused, then received, or did not receive, an apology. The blood pressure of the women who received an apology returned to normal quicker than the blood pressure of those who got no apology. Fascinating.

Men subjected to the same experiment, curiously, reacted in the opposite way – they just got get pissed off by the apology. So it seems as if the sexes speak a different emotional language here. But on which side of the sexual divide would you rather be? When did you last hear a woman say she wanted to get in touch with her masculine side?

Ultimately, we don't need to say sorry less or kick the whole apologising habit. We just need to say sorry *better*. And to do that, we need to obey certain basic rules. I won't trespass on readers' patience by drawing up an exhaustive list, a code of conduct for apologising, but here, with apologies for my presumption, are six simple precepts that could usefully be pinned on the wall of your bedroom/kitchen/office in Downing Street.

1. If you know you are at fault, say sorry.

This is the bottom line. It has to be. Keep a sense of proportion, obviously. Don't issue a galumphing elephant of an apology for a tiny mouse of a fault. The use of the s-word itself is not obligatory. Some other acknowledgement that you are at fault will suffice. But recognise the umbilical link between those two things: the original fault and the apology that needs to follow, in order for the fault to be purged. And if you are Sir Alex Ferguson or Ken Livingstone or Jeremy Clarkson, and following my precept involves saying sorry more than you normally would, don't shirk the challenge. Think of it as good exercise: keeping fit in the mental gym. Enjoy!

Step one, recognising when you are at fault, is simplicity itself. Modern science has shown us what a magnificently efficient creature *Homo sapiens* is, from his retentive brain to his miraculous hand-eye coordination. One of his most precious attributes, often overlooked, is his absolutely unerring conscience, as reliable as a Swiss watch or a Rolls-Royce engine. The wrong-doer *knows*, somewhere in his being, that he has done wrong. He may not always listen to the voice of conscience, but he hears it, every single time.

Of course, the voice of conscience can be hammering in your ears like a ghetto-blaster and the s-word still sticks in your throat. You dither. You prevaricate. You look ahead, second-guess the other person, calculate how they might react to your apology, chat to your PR people, engage a lawyer, play a waiting game. It is not hard to find a plausible excuse for not saying sorry – it is the easiest thing in the world – but there is nothing clever, or *macho,* or charming in falling back on excuses. Just think how irritated you get by the excuses which other people make. Ever had a plumber turn up three hours late, blaming traffic on the North Circular? Or had to listen to someone explain that they weigh 20 stone because they have the wrong sort of metabolism? Or shouted at the television as an MP explained that he shouldn't really have claimed for dog food but he was acting within the rules? *Remember* that irritation – then turn those memories to your advantage by not doing or saying anything that will risk irritating others.

Because you are going to be at fault a lot of times in your life, you are going to have to say sorry a lot of times. Get used to that; everyone is in the same boat. Which would you rather be – someone seen as too quick to apologise or someone who only apologises once in twenty years, through gritted teeth, after kicking and screaming like a baby? Your willingness to admit that you are not perfect is the guarantee of your humanity.

If you don't think you are at fault, don't say sorry for the sake of it just to keep someone else happy. That is the coward's way out; it devalues the currency. But for the currency to retain its value, the linkage between fault and apology needs to be retained, as a benchmark of how grown-up people should conduct themselves in a civilised society.

2. Say sorry sooner rather than later.

If revenge is a dish best served cold, an apology is best served warm: not piping hot, rushed straight from the oven to the table, but hot enough to keep its distinctive flavour, the bitter-sweet aroma of contrition. If you doubt that, just ask yourself two simple questions: How often have you heard someone apologise and thought, 'Too little, too late'? And how often have you heard someone apologise and thought, 'What, *already*? That's very sweet of you, but I'd rather you said sorry next week'? My case rests.

Of course, apologising promptly is easier said than done. When something is difficult, painful, or embarrassing, it is only human to delay doing it until the last possible minute, like a visit to the dentist. Up to a point, the person to whom you are apologising will understand that dynamic – they will have been in the same position themselves. But don't underestimate the damage that can be caused by delay or the appearance of delay. An unresolved row is a vacuum into which all kinds of noxious emotions can flow.

If you are living under the same roof as the person you have upset, it is easy to grasp the wisdom of a prompt apology. Making peace clears the air, stops things festering, and all that. But if you are a public figure, in disgrace for some reason, with the press camped outside your front door, the natural instinct is to lie low and wait until the storm has blown over. You know you are going to have to apologise at some point, but you assume that you have time on your side. Nothing could be further from the truth.

A day's worth of bad headlines quickly becomes a week's worth of bad headlines, and by the time you start trying to rebuild your reputation, you have a mountain to climb. It is far simpler to make an early unequivocal apology. The media circus will move on, they have got their pound of flesh, and, painful though it may be to give them their pound of flesh, you can move on, too. Whereas, if you just give them easy headlines with your apparent obstinacy . . . Journalists are the laziest pack animals on the planet.

Politicians fall into the same trap: trying to ride out storms when the situation calls for a different strategy. They take the long view of events; they fondly imagine themselves in retirement in Sussex, writing their memoirs, putting the record straight, admitting to a miscalculation here, a small error of judgement there; and they think that history will judge them on those memoirs, the fruit of mature reflection, not on their sound-bites for the *Sun* when they were ministers. History, frankly, has better things to do.

It is in the crucible of the here and now that political reputations are forged, and no single quality dents reputations more quickly than a lack of humility. Politician after politician gets something wrong – which, in the eyes of fair-minded voters, is normal and human and forgivable – and then voluntarily submits to double punishment: a caning for getting it wrong, then a second caning for refusing to *admit* they got it wrong.

In the bear-pit of the House of Commons, all they see is what is in front of them: Opposition MPs jeering and pointing and shouting 'Apologise!' They miss the bigger picture: all those millions of people out in the country who could not give a damn about party point-scoring, but just want their political leaders to do the best they can and, if they mess up, to *say so*.

For their own good, and not for reasons of altruism, politicians would be far better off owning up to their mistakes, and doing so as soon as reasonably possible. Instead, at times of stress they just freeze, like rabbits caught in the car headlights, fearing that if they admit to having got something wrong, their opponents will have a field day. But their opponents are going to have a field day anyway;

if they refuse point-blank to apologise they will give their opponents two field days.

So get your skates on, Dave, Gordon, Tony, Barack, Boris – whatever you are called –there is no time for shilly-shallying.

3. Do not wait for the other person to say sorry first.

This vital principle of apologising should be largely a matter of common sense, but it is extraordinary how few people grasp its significance.

Let us say A has had a row with B. Both A and B are reasonable, fair-minded people; they recognise that there has been fault on both sides and they are both prepared to apologise, in principle. But there is a small problem: A, having examined his conscience, concludes that, although he was at fault, B should accept slightly more of the blame – say, 60 per cent to his 40 per cent. B, having examined *his* conscience, reaches a rather different conclusion. He admits he has behaved badly, but thinks that, when everything is taken into account, it is A, not him, who should take 60 per cent of the blame. Result? A complete bloody *impasse*. Pistols at dawn.

Now it is easy to look at the bald arithmetic and conclude that, by iron mathematical logic, either A or B, or both, is guilty of dishonesty and a failure to accept full responsibility for their actions. But that would be a very narrow lens through which to view the situation. In the heat of the moment, to have a slightly distorted view of the events leading up to a row is a very human failing. What matters is not the arithmetic, but the emotional ambience. There is a deficit in good will, and that deficit needs to be addressed as a matter of urgency. If both A and B refuse to budge, declining to apologise unless the other one has apologised first, disaster looms.

So, put yourself in A's shoes. What is the most practical way to restore good will between yourself and B? Answer: *Say you are sorry for whatever it is you are sorry for.* You do not need to resile from your private conclusion that only 40 per cent of the row is your fault: you just need to say sorry for that 40 per cent, as it were, pinpointing something specific for which you are prepared to apologise, e.g., the fact that you have overreacted at some point in the row. B, being a reasonable man, will then apologise for his 40 per cent, and that will be that.

'But what about the outstanding 20 per cent?' I hear the pedant say. Gone. Dissolved. Vanished into thin air. As soon as good will is restored, the row is over, *finito*, and the blame game with it.

The beauty of this pragmatic approach to apologising is that it holds good even in circumstances where the apportionment of blame is more unequal. Suppose you are A and think that B is 80 per cent responsible for the row: you can *still* get in your apology first, accepting responsibility for your 20 per cent, and that will set the ball rolling. If B is a reasonable man, he will know, deep down, that he is the main culprit in the row, and match your apology with an even more generous one. He may do nothing of the kind, of course, in which case you are in trouble, and your relationship with B may never recover. But at least you will have tried. Blessed are the peace-makers . . .

4. When saying sorry, choose your words carefully.

With all the traps that lie in wait for the apologiser, the thousand tiny ways in which even the sincerest apology can strike the wrong note, the need for due diligence should be self-evident. Don't risk embarrassing yourself and irritating the other person by rushing out the first words of contrition that come into your head. Notwithstanding the importance of apologising promptly, you need to give proper thought to the wording. Professions of love write themselves, apologies have to be crafted.

Even though you are churning with emotion, you need to be hard-headed. What are you hoping to achieve with your apology? Are the words you have chosen likely to achieve that? Put yourself in the shoes of the intended recipient of the apology and try to hear your apology through their ears. Are they likely to be mollified by your words? Or will they just throw the apology back in your face?

More importantly, does the wording of your apology give due weight to the feelings of the person you have hurt, or is the apology self-serving? In most human transactions, people treat each other as equals, but an apology follows a different dynamic: one person is temporarily abasing themselves in front of another person, asking their forgiveness. Humility must be the keynote; there is no room in an apology for words that smack of vanity or bombast.

Depending on the complexity of the apology, it is not a bad idea to draft something, then leave it for an hour or two, or even sleep on it, before deciding on the final version. Read what you have written aloud and listen to how it sounds. Do some bits jar? Why do they jar? Try to diagnose the problem and come up with a solution.

If you are still not sure you have hit the right note, you might think of running your apology past a friend – but they will need to be an unusually sensitive friend, attuned to feelings as well as language. Apology-drafting should not be a council of war, thrashing out a face-saving strategy, planning how to beat a tactical retreat, it needs to involve real soul-searching.

Incidentally, if you are a public figure and know that your apology will be emblazoned across the front pages, take a few minutes imagining those front pages, and how your words will read when the *Daily Mirror* is being passed from hand to hand in the Dog and Duck in Melton Mowbray. What do you hear? Murmurs of approval? Voices saying, 'Good on him for doing the decent thing'? Or a chorus of guffaws? The wisdom of crowds can always pick a proper apology from a wrong 'un.

5. Err on the side of over-apologising rather than under-apologising.

Has anyone ever grumbled that a bunch of flowers you have given them is too big? Think of an apology as a bouquet and you are on the right track. Twelve roses are better than six, and twenty-four are better than twelve.

If the bunch-of-flowers analogy doesn't work for you, try the monkfish-and-chicory one. Suppose you have been to a dinner party and your hostess has served steamed monkfish with curried chicory on a bed of chopped spinach with a raspberry dressing, do you waste energy quibbling whether that combination of flavours works? Of course not, you are not a restaurant critic, so you just force the bloody food down and come up with the nicest compliment you can, consistent with not being a total hypocrite. The situation does not call for perfect frankness; it calls for generosity.

Of the seven deadly sins of apologising that I castigated earlier, almost all stem from the same basic fault: meanness of spirit. The apologisers are prepared to say sorry, but only on their own, highly restrictive, terms. No wonder their apologies sound so hollow. Don't fall into the same trap when crafting your own apologies.

A professional photographer once gave me a useful tip. When I was taking a photograph – whatever I was snapping, whether it was a cathedral, a flock of sheep or a group of drunken relatives at a wedding – I should set up the shot to my satisfaction, then take a full step forward before clicking the camera. In other words, I needed to make my subjects bigger if I wanted my photographs to have maximum impact. Overstatement was better than understatement; exaggeration was the key to truth. And it is the same with apologies. Draft and re-draft your apology until you are satisfied with it, then look for ways to beef it up slightly. Don't tone down the contrition – *magnify* the contrition. How exactly you do it depends on the apology: a simple 'very' before 'sorry' might be enough. Or perhaps you are admitting that you have behaved like an idiot? Would 'total idiot' be an improvement? You cannot just pump words into a sentence indiscriminately, but you can strengthen a sentence, in all kinds of tiny ways, until it delivers its intended message more forcefully.

People who habitually under-apologise pay a high price. Often the recipient of a half-hearted apology refuses to accept it, demanding further apologies, until an ugly tug-of-war develops. Cautious apologisers come across as dour, pedantic, tight-fisted. People make a mental note to avoid them, or not buy their records, or not vote for them. And, at the end of the day, these half-apologisers have only themselves to blame; they have had a chance to do something magnanimous and chivalrous, and they have blown it.

Apologisers who err on the side of generosity encounter no such difficulties; they not only make peace but enhance their reputation in the process. The very people who have been angry with them suddenly see them in a totally different light: sensitive rather than insensitive; self-critical rather than self-centred; courageous rather than cowardly. Out of the jaws of disaster, they have plucked a kind of triumph.

6. Say sorry in plain English.

This is a drum I have beaten so many times already that, if you have not heard the sound of the drum yet, you must work for that well-known firm of celebrity lawyers, Flannel, Flannel and Soap.

Strip most apologies down to their bare bones and something very, very simple is being said. 'I'm sorry I hurt you.' 'We got it wrong.' 'I chose my words badly.' 'We missed something we should have seen.' 'I didn't stop to think.' 'We let you down.' 'I cheated.' 'We betrayed your trust.' 'I acted like a two-year-old.' 'We ignored your needs.' 'I lied.' 'It won't happen again.' But how often do those words, the guts of the apology, survive into the final draft, after the apology has been cleared by the legal department and vetted by the press office? They are either replaced by longer words or surrounded by so much syntactical padding that you can hardly see them.

At other times in our lives, when we have important things to say, we instinctively use pared-down language: simple Anglo-Saxon words that have been around for centuries. In pillow talk, couples bare their souls to each other in monosyllables, not because they are inarticulate but because they know that, when you love someone, you have no need to resort to flowery language. It is the same with expressions of condolence; people make no effort to be Churchillian at such moments, they speak from the heart.

Any apology, verbal or written, should pass a very simple test: is it composed of words heard in everyday conversation, and *only* of such words? If it is not, it is probably already over-elaborate, putting distance between the apology and the feeling behind the apology. Even the kind of lofty sentiments that earn apologisers marks for effort – 'I apologise unconditionally' – are suspect. People in the high street do not use the word 'unconditionally' from one end of the year to the next, so when they hear it, they smell a rat; they worry that there are some conditions tucked away in the small print. 'I'm very sorry' has a far more authentic ring.

Of course, using plain English is harder than it seems. We live in a sophisticated age. We are in love with irony. We are used to trying to impress other people with our little verbal curlicues, the way we try to impress them with the accessories we wear. If we have had a good education, we like to show off that education – speaking in monosyllables feels like going around naked. But the fact that simplicity of expression goes against the grain only makes the search for it more challenging – and more rewarding when you get to your destination.

When you get an apology right, you know it straight away. You feel the same emotional buzz that you get when someone says sorry to you and their apology rings true as a bell. Your choice of words has helped connect you with a fellow human being, not put barriers of suspicion between you.

Life is good again – not because you have said sorry, but because you have said sorry in the right, authentic way, the way a child might. You have put sophistry and posturing behind you. You have mastered the hardest word of all.